COORDINATION
COMPOUNDS

COORDINATION COMPOUNDS

DEAN F. MARTIN
University of South Florida
BARBARA B. MARTIN

McGRAW-HILL BOOK COMPANY
New York   San Francisco   Toronto   London

COORDINATION COMPOUNDS

II

TO
W. C. F.

PREFACE

The chemistry of the coordination compounds is, in our opinion, an undeservedly neglected topic in a beginning chemistry course. It is treated piecemeal in most books, and the student is forced to await advanced courses for a unified treatment of the subject. This, in our view, is not a proper state of affairs.

Accordingly, we have written this book in order to present an introduction to the chemistry of coordination compounds at the beginning undergraduate level. The book is designed to serve as a supplementary text and to help overcome the awe that seems to surround this topic. It is our experience that the subject is of interest to students in beginning courses in chemistry and that much of the material presented herein is not beyond the mastery of beginning students. Obviously, some topics, such as ligand field theory, though very important in modern coordination chemistry, have been neglected in our treatment because of limitations of space and because of audience level. We have, however, provided references to pertinent articles so that the serious student can explore given topics. Also, it seems to us that students should have the benefits of an early exposure to the literature of chemistry.

It is a pleasure to acknowledge the inspiration of Professor John C. Bailar, Jr., and we are indebted to Professor Therald Moeller for his advice, encouragement, and helpful comments. Dr. W. Conard Fernelius, Professor Moeller, and William Randall have read the entire manuscript critically, and their criticisms have been most helpful. Not all of their suggestions have been followed, though, and whatever shortcomings remain in the book are the responsibility of the authors.

Dean F. Martin
Barbara B. Martin

CONTENTS

1

THE WORLD OF COORDINATION COMPOUNDS

1-1 AN INTRODUCTION TO A NEW AND AN OLD WORLD

The world of coordination compounds is a familiar, an unfamiliar, a new and an old world. Though this statement is seemingly paradoxical, it is nonetheless true. Coordination compounds are so ubiquitous that we cannot avoid encountering them; they are familiar to us, yet they remain unfamiliar because we ignore them or take them for granted. These compounds represent a world that is old in terms of its uses, new in terms of our understanding of it. The world of coordination compounds is a strange one, often resembling something out of a science-fiction novel.

Imagine a world of inhabitants so highly gregarious that they are unable to exist as individuals, so highly regimented that they exist in select groups of two, four, and six individuals surrounding a leader in highly symmetrical arrangements. Imagine a world of drab individuals and colorful crowds. In joining the crowd, the individuals lose their indentities, are influenced by, and in turn influence, the leader. Some groups of inhabitants are without a leader, but their standards are strict and their requirements quixotic; often they reject a leader solely on the basis of size or shape. The groups because of their association have special powers. They can capture a sunbeam, hold, and use it. They serve as blacksmiths and can forge vast chains. They can influence the course of other combinations and are useful for this power.

This analogy, while seemingly fantastic, does have a basis in fact. The leader is a metal ion and the individuals are molecules or ions which are arranged about the metal ion. Intensely colored dyes and pigments often result from the combination of relatively colorless metal ions and molecules. It is often found that certain molecules will arrange themselves about only those metal ions that meet highly specific requirements of size or charge. Such molecules are of great interest in analytical chemistry because of their great specificity. By virtue of their nature, coordination compounds have special properties. Chlorophylls, which are found in green plants, are able to use solar energy to convert carbon dioxide and water to starch and oxygen. Hemoglobin in blood is able to store, transfer, and later release oxygen. Other coordination compounds play important roles in biological processes, prevent the deterioration of rubber and other products, and serve to control the course of chemical reactions.

While coordination compounds are of great practical interest, they are also of theoretical interest. They represent a fundamental pattern of chemical combination which is common to all the materials mentioned previously and which is consistent with modern theory.

As a first step in understanding coordination compounds, we need to define some terms. In the broadest sense, a *coordination entity* may be defined* as a molecule or ion in which there is a metal atom or ion to which are closely attached other atoms (A) or

---

* This definition is based upon one suggested by the Commission on the Nomenclature of Inorganic Chemistry, International Union of Pure and Applied Chemistry.[1] (Superior numbers indicate References at the end of the chapter.)

groups (B). The metal atom is called the *central atom*, or *center of coordination*. The atoms directly attached to the central atom are called *coordinating atoms*, or *donor atoms*. Atoms (A) and groups (B) are referred to as *ligands*.

Thus, there are several features of a coordination entity. One is the metal ion (or occasionally atom), and, of course, the nature of the metal, its size, and the magnitude of its charge are important. A second feature is the ligand, which may be an atom, an ion (anion or, less commonly, a cation, e.g., $H_2NNH_3^+$), or a molecule. The third feature is the *coordination number*, i.e., the number of atoms attached to the central metal. Of course the geometry of the arrangement of the ligands is particularly important (see Chap. 3). Finally, the metal and the ligands surrounding it comprise the *coordination sphere*, which is conventionally represented by the bracket-enclosed symbols.

Many of the properties of coordination compounds are due to the ligand: the nature and the number of donor atoms and the charge on the ligand. The common donor atoms are nitrogen, oxygen, and sulfur. The ligand may contain one donor atom and be *unidentate*,* or the ligand may have two donor atoms and be *bidentate*. When the ligand contains two or more donor atoms, it is *multidentate* and is said to be a *chelate*.† The metal derivative is properly called a *metal-chelate compound*. When we look at Table 1-1, we see that the most obvious feature of the metal-chelate structure is the formation of a ring, usually of five or six members. Finally, the charge on the ligand is important because it determines many properties of the compound. If the sum of the negative charges of the ligands is equal to the charge on the metal

---

* One point of attachment; literally the group has "one tooth" (from *uni* plus *dens*).

† The adjective "chelate" was suggested by G. T. Morgan and H. D. K. Drew [*J. Chem. Soc.*, 117, 1456 (1920)] because of a fancied resemblance to the claw of a crab. The adjective was once limited to bidentate ligands, but is now universally applied to any multidentate ligand.

Table 1-1   EXAMPLES OF TERMS USEFUL IN UNDERSTANDING COORDINATION CHEMISTRY

Types of Coordination Compounds

Complex ion   *vs.*   *Metal-chelate compound**

$$\left[\begin{array}{c} NH_3 \\ \downarrow \\ H_3N \rightarrow Cu \leftarrow NH_3 \\ \uparrow \\ NH_3 \end{array}\right]^{++}$$

Tetraamminecopper(II) ion   Bis(glycinato)copper(II)

Types of Ligands

Unidentate   *vs.*   *Chelate*

NH_3, H_2O, CN^-, Cl^- Bidentate $CH_3\overset{O^-}{C}=CH\overset{O}{\overset{\|}{C}}CH_3$

Terdentate $HN(CH_2COO^-)_2$

Quadridentate $N(CH_2COO^-)_3$

Typical Ligands

Nitrogen donors: NH_3 Amines: RNH_2 (primary)

R_2NH (secondary)

R_3N (tertiary)

Oxygen donors: OH^-, H_2O, $RCOO^-$, ROH, R_2CO, $RCHO$

Donors related to nitrogen R_3As R_3P R_2S

and oxygen: arsines   phosphines   thioethers

Halide ions: F^-, Cl^-, Br^-, I^-

π-bonding ligands†: CN^- NCS^- CO

* Arrow indicates coordinate covalent bond.
† See page 70.

ion, the compound is a nonelectrolyte; otherwise it is an electrolyte.

The advantage, and the disadvantage, of the preceding definition of a coordination compound is that it is all-encompassing and includes any metal ion in water because the ion is surrounded by water molecules. It also includes many types of compounds

Table 1-2 FAMILIAR SUBSTANCES THAT ARE ACTUALLY
COORDINATION COMPOUNDS

Example	Representation	
Human blood (heme)	(N–M–N ring)*	$M = Fe^{II}$
Vitamin B_{12}	(N–M–N ring)	$M = Co^{III}$
Invertebrate animal blood (hemocyanin)	(N–M–N ring)	$M = Cu^{I}$
Chlorophyll	(N–M–N ring)	$M = Mg^{II}$
Silicates	$CaSiO_4$ or $Ca[SiO_4]$	
Hydrates	$Mg(ClO_4)_2 \cdot 6H_2O$ or $[Mg(H_2O)_6](ClO_4)_2$	
Hydroxides	$Al(OH)_3 \cdot 3H_2O$ or $[Al(OH)_3(H_2O)_3]$	
Ammoniates	$CuSO_4 \cdot 4NH_3$ or $[Cu(NH_3)_4]SO_4$	
Double salts	$Fe(CN)_2 \cdot 4NaCN$ or $Na_4[Fe(CN)_6]$	

* The structures that are represented are related to the metal phthalo-
cyanines (Fig. 1-3). All have the same essential feature, that is, they are metal
derivatives of a quadridentate ligand having four donor nitrogen atoms that
are joined in a ring.

such as hydrates, ammoniates, double salts, and double oxides, that are most conveniently regarded as examples of coordination compounds. Finally, it includes, of course, such diverse representatives of the animal, vegetable, and mineral kingdoms as blood, chlorophyll, and silicates, respectively (see Table 1-2). On the other hand, the definition says nothing about stability. For example, $NaCl \cdot 2NH_3$ exists only in contact with liquid ammonia or at low temperatures. In contrast, $K_3Fe(CN)_6$ is so stable that it does not give the usual reaction for ferric or cyanide ion, because too few of these ions are present.

1-2 FACTORS THAT INFLUENCE THE FORMATION OF COORDINATION COMPOUNDS

Now that we know what coordination compounds are, the next question that comes to mind is "Why do they form?" This is a question that has yet to be answered satisfactorily, because it is not an easy matter to understand the behavior of coordination entities. There are many simple rules and generalizations, but few work successfully in all cases. We can at least consider some of the factors involved. These include environmental factors such as temperature and pressure, and more important factors such as the nature of the metal ion and the nature of the ligand. The importance of each of these factors can be summarized as follows.

Environmental Factors: Temperature and Pressure

The effect of heat can be twofold. Volatile ligands may be lost at higher temperatures. This is exemplified by the loss of water by hydrates and by the loss of ammonia by $[Co(NH_3)_6]Cl_3$ on heating, though this complex ion is inert* in strongly acid solution:

$$[Co(NH_3)_6]Cl_3 \xrightarrow{175-180°C} [Co(NH_3)_5Cl]Cl_2 + NH_3$$

* Rigorously, it is necessary to make a distinction between "stability-instability" and "inertness-lability." Stability and instability are equilibrium

A second effect of temperature is the transformation of certain coordination compounds from one form to another. For example, Ag_2HgI_4 is reversibly transformed at 45°C from a red to a yellow form:

$$AgHg[AgI_4] \rightleftharpoons Ag_2[HgI_4]$$
$$\text{Red} \qquad \text{Yellow}$$

At this temperature, a shifting of ions occurs and two different structures are involved: one in which mercury is the central metal, and one in which the iodide ions surround a silver(I) ion.

The effect of pressure is ordinarily one of concentration. Since the formation of coordination compounds involves chemical equilibria, it is apparent that altering the pressure of volatile ligands is merely an application of the Le Chatelier principle. For example, solid $[Co(NH_3)_6]Cl_2$ loses ammonia upon heating but can be reformed by treatment of anhydrous cobalt(II) chloride with ammonia vapor.[3]

$$[Co(NH_3)_6]Cl_2 \overset{\Delta}{\rightleftharpoons} CoCl_2 + 6NH_3$$

The Metal

Several characteristics of the metal should be considered. These include intrinsic size and charge, electronic arrangement, and the size of the metal relative to that of the ligand. Some generalizations that have been observed follow.

Size and Charge. For a given ligand, the strength of the metal-ligand bond should depend upon the size of the ion and the magnitude of the ionic charge, and should be the greatest for small ions of high charge. These requirements are met by transition-metal ions, but not exclusively so. Beryllium(II) ion, which has a high charge-to-radius ratio, forms stable coordination compounds, especially when oxygen donor atoms are present. How-

---

or thermodynamic properties, whereas lability is a kinetic property. A labile complex is one that is very reactive and undergoes complete reaction within one minute at room temperature; an inert or robust complex is one that reacts at a rate too slow to measure or at a measurable rate.

ever, alkali metal ions also form metal-chelate compounds, though the stability of such compounds is not great.

In many ways, this simple picture is useful and satisfying, but it is also too simple because it is apparent that other factors are involved. For example, cadmium and calcium ions have the same charge-to-radius ratio, but the compounds of the former ion are far more stable. The ability of cobalt(II) and zinc(II) ions to form coordination compounds is not even approximately equal though both have a charge-to-radius ratio of 2.4. Other factors are involved, as will become evident later.

Electronic Configuration and Effective Atomic Number. The tendency of an atom to attain the electronic configuration of the nearest inert gas is well known. This end is achieved by transfer of one to three electrons (electrovalent bond) or by sharing (covalent bond). The latter is also observed for coordination compounds. An atom or ion may accept a share in a sufficient number of electrons, supplied by donor atoms, to have the electronic configuration or the *effective atomic number* (E.A.N.) of the next inert gas. The E.A.N. is equal to the number of electrons in the metal ion plus the number of electrons gained by coordination. For example, Co^{3+} in the complex ion $[Co(NH_3)_6]^{3+}$ has 24 electrons and effectively gains 12 electrons (two each from the six ammonia molecules). Thus, the E.A.N. of Co in $[Co(NH_3)_6]^{3+}$ is 36, the atomic number of the next inert gas, krypton.

The E.A.N. concept has been useful for rationalizing observed coordination numbers. The concept has been particularly successful with metal carbonyls.[3] Instability is suggested when the E.A.N. is one or two units greater or less than the atomic number of the next inert gas. Thus, the E.A.N. of cobalt in $[Co(CN)_6]^{4-}$ is 37 and this complex ion is readily oxidized to $[Co(CN)_6]^{3-}$ for which the E.A.N. is 36. A flaw in the concept is indicated by the observation that $[Fe(CN)_6]^{4-}$ (E.A.N. of Fe = 36) is slowly oxidized by air to $[Fe(CN)_6]^{3-}$ (E.A.N. of Fe = 35). There are a number of other exceptions to the E.A.N. generalization.[3]

Size of the Metal, Size of the Ligand, the Radius Ratio.
We should expect to find that the relative sizes of the ligand and
metal ion are important in determining the number of ligands that
can be accommodated around the metal ion. If the ligand is
exceptionally large or if the metal ion is exceptionally small, fewer
ligands can be arranged about the metal than would be possible
with optimum sizes (Fig. 1-1). In other words, there are several
limiting radius ratios (radius of central atom to radius of ligand)
which determine the coordination number of the metal ion. These
are summarized in Table 1-3. Generally, the agreement between

Table 1-3   *RADIUS RATIO AND COORDINATION NUMBER*

Formula	Radius ratio $= \dfrac{\text{radius M}}{\text{radius A}}$	Coordination number	Arrangement*
MA_2	0–0.15	2	Collinear
MA_3	0.15–0.22	3	Triangular plane
MA_4	0.41–0.59	4	Planar
MA_4	0.22–0.41	4	Tetrahedral
MA_6	0.41–0.59	6	Octahedral

* Cf. page 46.

observed and predicted coordination number is very good for
oxygen coordination.

The Ligand

In theory, a ligand is any ion or molecule which has some atom
capable of electron donation, usually of a so-called lone pair of
electrons. In practice, the number of donor atoms is quite limited,
and the coordination tendencies of ligands vary from nil to great.
In discussing the donor atoms we need to keep in mind several
factors, including the nature of the donor atom, the group of which

it is a part (i.e., unidentate vs. multidentate), and the steric requirements of the metal vs. those of the ligand.

The Donor Atom. A number of typical ligands are listed in Table 1-1. A comparatively few elements serve as donor atoms; many do not because of unfavorable size or electronic effects. Many elements which might function as donor atoms have not

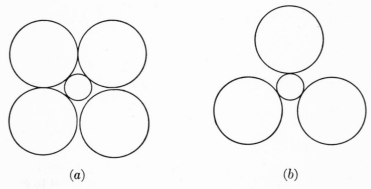

(a)   (b)

FIGURE 1-1   The radius ratio concept showing an unfavorable situation (a) (large ligand, small ion) in which the maximum coordination number is not attained because of ligand-ligand interaction. The favorable situation (b) (large ligand, small ion) results when ligand-ligand interaction is reduced because of fewer ligands.

been fully investigated. Some, such as sulfur, arsenic, and selenium, form compounds which are sufficiently obnoxious, toxic, or difficult to prepare to discourage most chemists.

The relationship between the donor and acceptor atoms has been summarized elsewhere,[2] but it may be noted that a number of metals show definite preference for a given donor atom. Also, some metals show definite preference for certain members of a set of related ligands. For example, the fluoride complexes of aluminum(III) are the most stable and the best characterized of the aluminum-halogen complexes, but the halide complexes of the related thallium(III) ion are limited to those of chlorine, bromine, and iodine.[2]

The unsaturated ligands listed in Table 1-1 are especially interesting. Some of the compounds involving double-bonded ligands, e.g., Zeise's salt, $K[PtCl_3C_2H_4]$, have been known since the beginning of the nineteenth century. However, the nature of the bonding has become clarified only within recent years.

Unidentate vs. Multidentate. The formation of rings by chelate or multidentate ligands when combined with a metal ion results in greatly enhanced stability. Although it is not practicable to list here all of the chelates that are known, many types have been listed by Diehl.[4] We can think of chelates as being made up of unidentate ligands. For example, methylamine, CH_3NH_2, is just about one-half of the chelate ethylenediamine, $H_2NCH_2CH_2NH_2$. Also, the anion of an amino acid, $RCH(NH_2)COO^-$, is a stronger coordinating agent than its "components," a primary amine, RNH_2, and the anion of carboxylic acid, $RCOO^-$. The picture of chelating agents as being composed of unidentate ligands is not always correct. For example, acetone, $(CH_3)_2C{=}\overset{..}{O}:$, does not form stable complex ions, nor does the chelate

$$CH_3COCH_2CH_2COCH_3$$

but an alternative combination, acetylacetonate ion,

$$CH_3COCHCOCH_3^-,$$

does form stable metal derivatives.

Acetylacetone is an interesting compound which exists in two forms, called the enol and the keto:

Enol   Keto

The enol form can lose a proton, react with a metal ion, and thus form a metal-chelate compound, which we represent as

The physical properties of these compounds are often those of organic materials rather than metal salts, as indicated by the

Table 1-4   *PHYSICAL PROPERTIES OF*
              TRIS(2,4-PENTANEDIONO)CHROMIUM(III)[*,†]

	Temp., °C	Other properties
Melting point	216	Red-violet, crystalline
Boiling point	ca. 340	Very soluble in benzene
Partial sublimation as low as	100	Insoluble in water

* W. C. Fernelius and J. E. Blanch, *Inorganic Syntheses*, **5**, 130 (1957).
† W. C. Fernelius and B. E. Bryant, *Inorganic Syntheses*, **5**, 105–113 (1957).

properties of chromium acetylacetonate (M = Cr; n = 3) listed in Table 1-4. The stability of this compound is illustrated by the fact that it can be distilled at such a high temperature.

Steric Requirements of the Ligand. Very often the steric requirements of the ligand are not compatible with the normal

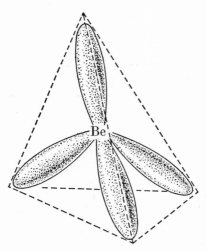

FIGURE 1-2 Beryllium in preferred tetrahedral configuration.

configuration of the metal. A coordination compound may be formed, but not willingly, as it were. The situation is known as a *forced configuration*, and it represents a Procrustean bed of chemistry.

The outstanding examples of this are the metal derivatives of phthalocyanine, which is a planar, quadridentate ligand. The bonds between the metal and this ligand should lie in a plane, but metals such as beryllium which normally have bonds directed at the corners of a tetrahedron (Fig. 1-2) do form complexes with phthalocyanine (Fig. 1-3).

The preceding example might suggest that the spatial arrange-

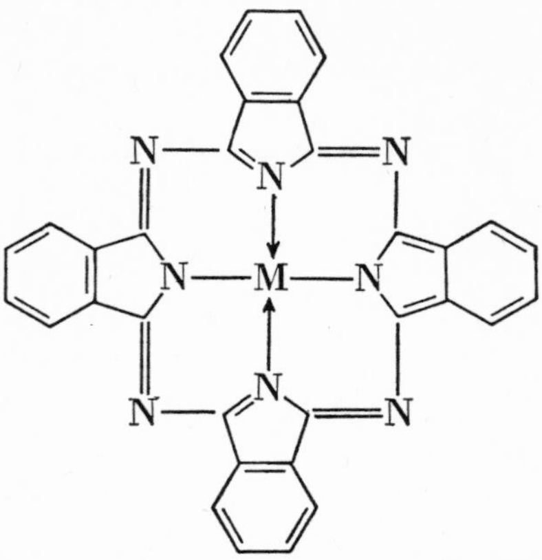

FIGURE 1-3   Metal phthalocyanine complex.

ment of the metal bonds simply changes to conform to the ligand requirements, but this is not accurate. A sounder view is that the bonds are distorted from the normal, optimum situation as a result of stress. If the strain imposed by the requirements of the ligand is too severe, either distortion will occur or a forced configuration will not exist. Platinum(II) and palladium(II) complexes are normally planar. The platinum(II) and palladium(II) derivatives of β,β',β''-triaminotriethylamine (abbreviated "tren"), $N(CH_2CH_2NH_2)_3$, should have a tetrahedral arrangement of bonds (Fig. 1-4), if all four nitrogen atoms are attached to the same metal atom. It is now generally concluded that in these compounds forced configuration does not exist. Rather, one coordination position is occupied by a water molecule or an atom belonging to another ligand.*

* An alternate arrangement has been observed for [Ni(tren)](NCS)₂. The ligand occupies four positions of a regular octahedron with two anions in the remaining positions. [D. Hall and M. D. Woulfe, *Proc. Chem. Soc.*, **346** (1958).]

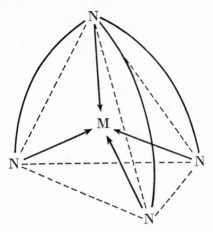

FIGURE 1-4   Schematic representation of tetrahedral structure of $[Mtren]^{++}$.

The silver(I) diamine complexes of the type

$$
\left[
\begin{array}{c}
Ag \\
H_2N \diagup \quad \diagdown NH_2 \\
H_2C \qquad\qquad CH_2 \\
\diagdown (CH_2)_n \diagup
\end{array}
\right]^{+}
$$

represent an interesting example of another way in which strain can be relieved. The compounds for which n is 1, 2, and 3 are more stable in solution than the ethylenediamine derivative $(n = 0)$. Since the two coordinate bonds of silver(I) are normally linear, there is much less distortion when higher-membered rings are formed. The strain is sufficiently great with ethylenediamine that this ligand does not behave as a chelate but instead apparently forms short chains as well as rings of the type[5]

$$
\begin{array}{c}
\mathrm{H_2} \;\;{}_{+}\;\; \mathrm{H_2} \\
\mathrm{N{\rightarrow}Ag{\leftarrow}N} \\
\mathrm{H_2C} \qquad\qquad \mathrm{CH_2} \\
\mathrm{H_2C} \qquad\qquad \mathrm{CH_2} \\
\overset{+}{\mathrm{N{\rightarrow}Ag{\leftarrow}N}} \\
\mathrm{H_2} \qquad \mathrm{H_2}
\end{array}
$$

1-3 THE NOMENCLATURE OF COORDINATION COMPOUNDS

At this point, now that we know something about these compounds, it is useful to be able to name them.

Initially, the structures of coordination compounds were unknown, and so a compound was usually named after the man who first reported it. For example, *Zeise's salt* has been mentioned. The problem which arises when the early chemist prepared more than one compound was solved in a simple way: *Rieset's first chloride, Rieset's second chloride.* Logically, *Cleve's first salt* (note the noncommittal approach) was followed by *Cleve's second salt,* but a more imaginative and descriptive approach is suggested by *Magnus's pink salt* and *Magnus's green salt.* Although these names indicate the activity of the chemist, they convey little chemical information.*

Fremy brought some order out of this chaos in 1840 with his suggestion that the cobalt ammines be given names suggestive of their colors. Since he had a good background in classical languages, the latinate names were used. This system later degenerated so that the *luteo* (yellow) series, for example, was used to refer to compounds of the type $M(NH_3)_6$ even though many such compounds are not yellow.[2]

* The formulas of some complex compounds named after their discoverers or colors have been summarized by Bailar and Busch.[2]

The present system of nomenclature is derived from one suggested by Alfred Werner (page 29) whose system satisfied many of the needs of nomenclature: the name and oxidation state of the metal, the number and nature of the ligands, and the ions present outside the coordination sphere. The Stock system is now used to designate oxidation state. Only these essential features can be described here, but further details and background can be found elsewhere.[1,6]

There are certain steps that are followed in naming these compounds.

1. As in simple salts, the name of the cation is given first.

2. The contents of the coordination sphere are specified: first the ligands, then the metal.

   a. The nature of the ligands is indicated by a suffix: positively charged ligands have the suffix *-ium*, neutral ligands no suffix, and negative ligands usually have the suffix *-o* (but H_2O and NH_3 are called *aquo* or *aqua* and *ammine*, respectively).

   b. The ligands are named in a definite order according to their charge: anionic ones first, then neutral, then cationic. Conventionally, but according to some not conveniently, the names are not separated by spaces or hyphens.

   c. The number (two, three, four) of each kind of ligand is indicated by prefixes, *di-, tri-, tetra-* (for ligands having simple names such as chloro), or *bis-, tris-,* or *tetrakis-* (for ligands having complicated names such as 2,4-pentanediono).

   d. Finally, the name of the metal is given, the oxidation state indicated by a Roman numeral in parentheses, and the nature of the coordination sphere indicated by the suffix *-ate* for an anionic complex or no suffix for cationic or neutral complexes.

Some examples of the naming of typical compounds are listed in Table 1-5.

Table 1-5 EXAMPLES OF THE NOMENCLATURE OF
COORDINATION COMPOUNDS

Formula	Name
[PtCl₂(NH₃)₄]Br₂	Dichlorotetraammineplatinum(IV) bromide
[Al(OH)₂(H₂O)₄]⁺	The dihydroxotetraaquoaluminum(III) ion
[Co(NO₂)(NH₃)₅]SO₄	Nitropentaamminecobalt(III) sulfate
[Co(ONO)(NH₃)₅]SO₄	Nitritopentaamminecobalt(III) sulfate
[Co(H₂NCH₂CH₂NH₂)₃]Cl₃	Tris(ethylenediamine)cobalt(III) chloride
NH₄[Cr(NCS)₄(NH₃)₂]	Ammonium tetrathiocyanatodiammine-chromate(III)
Na₃[Fe(CN)₆]	Sodium hexacyanoferrate(III)
Na₃[Co(NO₂)₆]	Sodium hexanitrocobaltate(III)
[Zr(CH₃COCHCOCH₃)₄]	Tetrakis(2,4-pentanediono)zirconium(IV)

The Formula column:

[PtCl$_2$(NH$_3$)$_4$]Br$_2$
[Al(OH)$_2$(H$_2$O)$_4$]$^+$
[Co(NO$_2$)(NH$_3$)$_5$]SO$_4$
[Co(ONO)(NH$_3$)$_5$]SO$_4$
[Co(H$_2$NCH$_2$CH$_2$NH$_2$)$_3$]Cl$_3$
NH$_4$[Cr(NCS)$_4$(NH$_3$)$_2$]
Na$_3$[Fe(CN)$_6$]
Na$_3$[Co(NO$_2$)$_6$]
[Zr(CH$_3$COCHCOCH$_3$)$_4$]

1-4 USES OF COORDINATION COMPOUNDS

Frequently in early times, a need was met by the use of a coordination compound, but the role of the compound in meeting this need has often been clear only in modern times. In certain instances the role of a compound is obscure and in need of clarification. Many uses have been found only recently, and others remain to be discovered. At this point, we shall merely list and sketch some of these uses.

Dyes

The characteristic colors of coordination compounds would indicate their utility as dyes. This use was discovered accidentally in ancient times (page 25), but dyeing was, and perhaps still is, an art rather than a science. Alfred Werner demonstrated the relation of coordination and dyeing when he showed[7] that several compounds which were capable of forming metal-chelate compounds were able to dye cloth pretreated with ferric hydroxide. The first complete studies of coordination compounds as dyes was undertaken by the English chemist G. T. Morgan and his co-workers in the early 1920s.

Since Morgan's work, most studies have been concerned with the interaction of dye, metal, and ligands present in the fiber. A number of man-made fibers pose special problems in dyeing because of the lack of certain groups or ligands which are a part of natural fibers.

Ion Control

There are many situations in which it is desirable or necessary to be able to control the concentration of metal ions by physical removal or by sequestration,[8] which is the suppression of a property or a reaction of a metal ion without the removal of the metal from solution. Thus, the metal is for all intents and purposes "removed" without being physically removed. This end can be achieved through the formation of coordination compounds. Some examples will help to point up the diversity and importance of this application.

In qualitative analysis, a mixture of cadmium and copper ions is separated by treating an alkaline solution of the two ions with cyanide ion and then precipitating cadmium as cadmium sulfide. The separation depends upon the fact that $[Cd(CN)_4]^=$ is less stable than $[Cu(CN)_3]^=$.

$$Cu^{++} \underset{}{\overset{CN^-}{\rightleftharpoons}} [Cu(CN)_3]^=$$

$$Cd^{++} \underset{}{\overset{CN^-}{\rightleftharpoons}} [Cd(CN)_4]^=$$

Metal ions, even though present in minute quantities, often cause undesired reactions, as in the Raschig synthesis of hydrazine, H_2NNH_2. The yield of hydrazine is greatly reduced if copper ion is present because of a metal-catalyzed side reaction. Glue has been added to remove copper and other metal ions, presumably through chelation. A much better practice is the addition of a pure chelating agent, tetrasodium ethylenediaminetetraacetate, EDTA,

$$Na_4 \begin{bmatrix} OOCCH_2 \quad\quad CH_2COO \\ \\ NCH_2CH_2N \\ \\ OOCCH_2 \quad\quad CH_2COO \end{bmatrix}$$

Often, large quantities of a metal ion must be removed. The outstanding example of this is the removal of calcium ion in water softening through the addition of chelates, e.g., polyphosphates, that form water-soluble calcium compounds.

A different aspect of ion control is that of ion analysis for which the quantitative reaction of a ligand with a metal ion is necessary. The amount of the coordination compound that is formed might be determined by direct weighing, if the substance is insoluble, or colorimetrically since the intensity of the color of a solution of a complex ion is related to its concentration. Mixtures of ions are frequently encountered in chemical analysis, and it is desirable to have a collection of ligands that will remove only specific metal ions from such a mixture. This is equivalent to having a set of chemical tweezers. The first example of a number of such tweezers was dimethylglyoxime, $CH_3C(=NOH)C(=NOH)CH_3$. This compound forms a red, insoluble nickel(II) salt and is specific for this ion and for palladium(II) ion. The formula of the nickel compound is shown below (dotted lines indicate hydrogen bonding).

Finally, control of ion activity in a given reaction may be involved. A ligand is added ostensibly to reduce the ion concentration, but often the effectiveness is because the coordination compound undergoes the desired reaction more readily than the free metal ion. Many examples of this are found in electroplating. A particularly interesting example is the use of cyanide ion in silverplating. It has been assumed that the function of the complex involved, $[Ag(CN)_2]^-$, is to provide a very low concentration of silver ion because of a slight tendency to dissociate.

$$[Ag(CN)_2]^- \rightleftharpoons Ag^+ + 2CN^-$$

Since the concentration of silver ion is never great, the reduction of the silver ion occurs very slowly to provide a smooth surface. Although this is a reasonable view, a summary of the evidence does not support it.[9] On the contrary, silver metal is formed by direct reduction of $[Ag(CN)_2]^-$.

As Catalysts

Some years ago, there was a sudden interest in the role of coordination compounds when it was discovered that some could influence the course of polymerization so as to provide plastics having desirable properties including higher softening temperatures and greater strength. The greater strength is indicated by the fact that the "safety" helmets worn by construction workers are now made of plastic.

Many enzymes, which serve as the catalysts in living systems, are coordination compounds. For example, the decomposition of hydrogen peroxide is catalyzed by many things, including iron compounds.

$$2H_2O_2 \xrightarrow{\text{catalyst}} 2H_2O + O_2$$

Ordinary hydrated ferric ion has a relative catalytic activity of 1; a coordination compound of iron, the heme (cf. Table 1-2), has a relative activity of one thousand; and catalase, a heme surrounded by a complicated protein structure, has a relative catalytic activity of ten billion.[10]

Finally, there are many examples of chemical reactions that involve the formation of coordination compounds which undergo subsequent reaction.[11] One significant example of this is the formation of α-nitro acids by combination of carbon dioxide and nitroparaffins.[12]

$$RNO_2 + CO_2 \xrightarrow{Mg(OC_2H_5)_2} R-\underset{\underset{O}{\overset{\diagdown}{\underset{N}{\parallel}}}{}}{C}-COO \xrightarrow{H^+} \underset{NO_2}{\overset{Mg}{RC}}-COOH + Mg^{++}$$

Interestingly enough, the reverse reaction occurs in weakly basic solution.

By now we are aware of the world of coordination compounds and its significance. Historically, the discovery of these compounds was a very gradual process, as we shall see in the next chapter.

REFERENCES

1. J. Am. Chem. Soc., 82, 5523 (1960).
2. J. C. Bailar, Jr., and D. H. Busch, in "The Chemistry of the Coordination Compounds" (J. C. Bailar, Jr., ed.), Reinhold Publishing Corporation, New York, 1956, chap. 1.
3. R. W. Parry and R. N. Keller, in "The Chemistry of the Coordination Compounds" (J. C. Bailar, Jr., ed.), Reinhold Publishing Corporation, New York, 1956, chap. 3.
4. H. Diehl, Chem. Rev., 21, 39 (1937).
5. G. Schwarzenbach et al., Helv. Chim. Acta, 35, 2337 (1952).
6. W. C. Fernelius, Advan. Chem. Ser., 8, 9 (1953).
7. A. Werner, Ber., 41, 1062 (1908).

8. R. L. Smith, "The Sequestration of Metals," Chapman & Hall, Ltd., London, 1959.
9. R. W. Parry and E. H. Lyons, Jr., in "The Chemistry of the Coordination Compounds" (J. C. Bailar, Jr., ed.), Reinhold Publishing Corporation, New York, 1956, p. 627.
10. M. Calvin, *Perspectives Biol. Med.*, 5, 399 (1962).
11. A. E. Martell and M. Calvin, "Chemistry of the Metal Chelate Compounds," Prentice-Hall, Inc., Englewood Cliffs, N.J., 1952, chap. 8.
12. M. Stiles and H. L. Finkbeiner, *J. Am. Chem. Soc.*, 81, 505 (1959).

2

THE YEARS OF
DISCOVERY

2-1 A COLORFUL BEGINNING

Coordination compounds were used long before they were recognized as such. The discovery of coordination compounds by chemists was made shortly after the French Revolution, and the understanding of them began, properly, with Werner's coordination theory late in the nineteenth century and parallels the ever-increasing understanding of chemistry in general.

The origin of coordination compounds is ill-defined. Certainly, one of the initial uses was as dyes and pigments, and it is interesting to trace the history of alizarin dye, which was prepared from madder and clay. Madder is the root of *Rubia tinctorum*, a plant found in various parts of Europe, the British Isles, and Asia Minor. We know now that alizarin dye is a calcium aluminum (ions present in clay) complex of hydroxyanthraquinone (from madder):

Madder dye was used in several areas of the ancient world, and aside from its use as a dye it was evidently used medicinally, since it colors red the bones of animals fed upon it. This effect appears to be due to the coordination of madder with the calcium in bone. Madder-base dyes are also a part of our history.[1] Every American has read of the "Redcoats," the polite colloquial term for the British army of the Revolutionary period. These red coats worn by the soldiers were dyed with madder, as were the "pinks" worn by fox hunters from the time of Henry II.

Coordination compounds, specifically madder-clay materials, were involved in what was surely the first example of chemical warfare.[1]* The use of the red dye described above permitted the Macedonians under Alexander the Great to defeat a much larger Persian force, who attacked heedlessly at dawn of the second day of a decisive battle. It seemed the opportune time to destroy the Macedonians, whose bloodstained garments showed that many had been wounded during the previous day's fighting, and that few had received medical care. The subsequent defeat of the Persians was due in large measure to their lack of caution. They did not realize that the wily Alexander had dyed the tunics of most of his men with bloodlike splotches.

2-2   THE YEARS OF DISCOVERY

The preceding represents only a few examples of the early uses of coordination compounds. Chemists became aware of these compounds when Tassaert observed in 1798 that cobalt salts combine with ammonia. After this discovery, much experimental work was done by various chemists to try to determine how such compounds were to be explained. For example, many studies were made on the cobalt(III) chlorides containing various amounts of ammonia and/or water. Conductivity studies gave an indication of the num-

* This material was adapted with permission from *J. Chem. Educ.*, **37**, 220 (1960).

ber of ions present in solutions of these salts, and treatment with silver nitrate indicated two types of chlorines. Typical data are listed in Table 2-1. Information from these studies and similar ones

Table 2-1 CHEMICAL AND PHYSICAL PROPERTIES OF
AMMONIA–COBALT(III) CHLORIDE COMPOUNDS

| Compound | Color | Ions/mole in aqueous solution | | Formula |
		Total (conductance)	Ionic Cl⁻* (AgCl ppt.)	
$CoCl_3 \cdot 6NH_3$	Yellow-orange	4	3	$[Co(NH_3)_6]Cl_3$
$CoCl_3 \cdot 5NH_3 \cdot H_2O$	Pink	4	3	$[Co(NH_3)_5H_2O]Cl_3$
$CoCl_3 \cdot 5NH_3$	Violet	3	2	$[Co(NH_3)_5Cl]Cl_2$
$CoCl_3 \cdot 4NH_3$	Violet	2	1	†cis-$[Co(NH_3)_4Cl_2]Cl$
$CoCl_3 \cdot 4NH_3$	Green	2	1	$trans$-$[Co(NH_3)_4Cl_2]Cl$

* Cl⁻ outside coordination sphere.
† Cf. page 48.

on other types of salts gave several chemists a large amount of data from which to formulate theories to explain these strange compounds and observations.

There is an understandable tendency on the part of many to attribute to Werner a full-blown, neatly packaged theory which explained all of the observed facts. Actually, the development of the theory was preceded by many years in which various proposals were set forth only to be rejected in favor of others. This contentious period has been described in detail by others,[2,3] and only the salient features need be mentioned here.

Certain proposals apparently served as a background for Werner, and others had features that were incorporated into his theory. For example, the proposals made by Claus in the 1850s were vigorously opposed by other workers. Yet, parts of the Claus proposals appeared 40 years later with only slight modifications as part of Werner's proposals, which have been generally accepted. Claus believed that ammonia, upon association with a metal chloride, somehow lost its basic character and was in a state differing from that usual in ammonium salts. The suggestion that the ammonia had become a "passive" molecule was not accepted. Claus believed that the factors which determined the number of molecules of ammonia that were united with a metallic salt would also apply to water molecules. This proposal was open to attack because of the lack of appropriate examples, but the suggestion became an accepted part of Werner's theory.

Another major development was made in 1871 when Blomstrand suggested a chain theory based upon a logical, but incorrect, analogy with organic amines. It was assumed that a metallic atom or ion could replace the hydrogen atoms of ammonia just as organic moieties do in the formation of amines such as CH_3NH_2, $(CH_3)_2NH$, and $(CH_3)_3N$. For example, the existence of two forms of $PtCl_4(NH_3)_2$ was rationalized by the two formulas

$$Cl_3Pt—NH_3—NH_3Cl$$

and

$$Cl_2Pt(NH_3Cl)_2$$

The chain theory was accepted and extended by S. M. Jörgensen. It is of interest mainly because it became a matter of contention between Jörgensen and Werner. This contention provided the stimulus for research, and, as more experimental data became available, the theory required increasing modification. Ultimately the much-patched theory was discarded, but it had a long period of popularity despite its flaws.

In 1891, Alfred Werner, at the age of twenty-five, published a paper entitled "Contribution to the Theory of Affinity and Valence," in which he rejected the usual concepts of valence and affinity, or attraction, of atoms for one another. The following year, Werner established the coordination theory, which formed the foundation for a new field of inorganic chemistry.

2-3 WERNER, THE MAN AND THE THEORY

Before considering Werner's theory in some detail, it might be well to describe the man who produced this theory. Alfred Werner was born in Alsace in 1866 and, after attending the lower schools and serving a term in the army, moved to Zurich in 1886 where he received his excellent chemical training. At the age of twenty-nine he was appointed a full professor at the University of Zurich, a position he held until 1919, the year of his death.

Werner has been described[4] as being a sincere, candid man, but at the same time a master who demanded of his pupils and associates the same determination and endurance which he possessed. He regularly discussed the chemical literature and his own investigations. Since he had a remarkable memory which covered the whole field of chemistry (defined at that time as inorganic and organic), his associates often had difficulty following him, much less trying to contribute to the discussions, as he demanded.

Werner was a comparatively informal and casual person, as indicated by an incident involving Paul Pfeiffer.[5] Another well-known research director at Zurich required that prospective students introduce themselves to him, while Werner permitted the introduction to be made by a third person. Pfeiffer described himself as being so shy that the prospect of introducing himself to anyone was overwhelming. Consequently, he had himself introduced to Werner, and the two began a long and fruitful collaboration.

Pfeiffer says in regard to Werner's formulation of the coordination theory, "According to his own statement, the inspiration came to him like a flash. One morning at two o'clock he awoke with a start: the long-sought solution of this problem had lodged in his brain. He arose from his bed and by five o'clock in the afternoon the essential points of the coordination theory were achieved."[4]*

In developing his theory and postulates, Werner made two marked departures from prevailing theory. First, he discarded chain theory in favor of a sort of monarchical principle or a centralized construction. This conception focused attention on a central atom about which other atoms arranged or coordinated themselves. This in itself was not new; about 1860, Kolbe had tried to apply the monarchical pattern to organic compounds, but the lack of "privileged" or central atoms doomed the attempt to failure. Secondly, it was inevitable that Werner deviate from the valence theory of his day because it was inadequate for his purposes.

Since attention was focused on the central atom, Werner logically began with the concept of the valence of that atom. Valence, it should be recalled, is a property of an atom which determines the number of other atoms to which the first atom may be bound. In Werner's time, it was thought that the valence of an atom was invariable, that it was a fundamental property as constant as atomic weight. Werner pointed out, however, that valences, or "saturation capacities,"† of certain elements depend upon the nature of those elements with which they are in combination. Moreover, the valence of an atom is variable and is not an inherent property of the atom.

When Werner next considered compounds of higher order, or complex compounds, the concept of valence, even allowing valence to be variable, could not be used to explain the formation and for-

---

* By permission from *J. Chem. Educ.*, **5**, 1090 (1928).

† Most chemists of the Werner period thought that the combining power of atoms was due to the affinity between the atoms. The valence represented a numerical measure of this affinity. Some molecules (for example, NH_3) were able to undergo further reaction, and this was taken as proof that not all of the affinity had been "saturated." In short, there were still free valences, or the "saturation capacity" had not been reached.

mulas of addition compounds (e.g., $O_3S + OH_2 = O_3S \cdot OH_2$), ammonia compounds, such as $PtCl_4 \cdot 2NH_3$, and hydrates.

Werner devised new structural formulas, for which he proposed the name "coordination formulas," and announced a new principle governing the combining possibilities of the atom. This was that an atom, even when its combining possibilities (primary valence) are exhausted according to the doctrine of valence, still possesses a peculiar kind of affinity which enables it to form molecular complexes. For this affinity he proposed the term "auxiliary valence." This principle is the fundamental postulate of Werner's coordination theory.

The distinction between auxiliary and primary valences was not clear initially. Ultimately, Werner recognized that there was merely a formal distinction between the two. Possibly he recognized this at an early stage because he noted the analogy between metal ammines and the ammonium ion. The structure of the latter was usually represented as involving equivalent bonds and a pentavalent nitrogen, e.g.,

$$\begin{array}{c} H \\ | \\ H-N-H \\ / \quad \backslash \\ H \quad\quad Cl \end{array}$$

Werner knew nothing about a lone pair of electrons on the nitrogen, but he did overcome this flaw of contemporary valence theory and represented the compound as we now do, $[NH_4]Cl$. He postulated that three primary valences bound the hydrogen atoms in ammonia and that a secondary valence held the fourth hydrogen. Werner recognized that there is no difference between the primary and secondary valences once the ammonium ion is formed. While he drew an analogy between ammonium ion and metal ammines, its full significance was not immediately apparent to others, and the formulation of ammonium salts with pentavalent nitrogen continued for decades after Werner's correct suggestion.[3]

The number of atoms or groups directly attached to an atom (either by primary or auxiliary valences) Werner called the *coordination number* of the atom. He found that only a few coordination numbers are prevalent, namely two, four, six, and eight, with six by far the most common. Werner proposed likely spatial configurations for these coordination numbers; explained the existence of geometrical isomers; and predicted the existence of optical isomers, which he eventually isolated, for some compounds of coordination number 6 (page 50). These were the first known optically active inorganic compounds.

It is interesting to see how these postulates can be, and were, used to explain the properties of the cobalt(III) chloride–ammonia complexes listed in Table 2-1. The metal ion and the coordinated species comprise the coordination sphere (now represented by brackets). The data show that there are two types of chlorines; those that are readily available are not a part of the coordination sphere. Thus, the compound $CoCl_3 \cdot 6NH_3$ would be represented as $[Co(NH_3)_6]Cl_3$ since there are three readily available chloride ions; and in solution, four ions, $[Co(NH_3)_6]^{3+}$ and three chloride ions, would be expected and are found.

The formulas for the other compounds can be determined in a similar way and are listed in Table 2-1. Two compounds, a violet and a green form of $CoCl_3 \cdot 4NH_3$, are puzzling because they have the same formula though they are obviously different. These are respectively the *cis* and *trans* forms of geometrical isomers (page 48) and their existence is a consequence of the spatially directed secondary valences (Fig. 2-1). The six coordinated atoms are at the corners of an octahedron.

As might be expected, Werner's radical departure from long-accepted theories and concepts met with disapproval and controversy. Jörgensen in particular criticized Werner's theory on several points: the postulate that all coordinating groups occupy equivalent positions in the coordination sphere, Werner's designation of isomers of such compounds as $[CoCl_2(NH_3)_4]Cl$, and the prediction of compounds which were then unknown. Jörgensen also felt that a negative coordinated ion could not lower the charge of the complex, since, it seemed to him, a group could not saturate both a primary and an auxiliary valence.

These criticisms and others, both sound and unsound, caused Werner and his associates to produce experimental evidence to support the coordination theory in almost every detail.* The

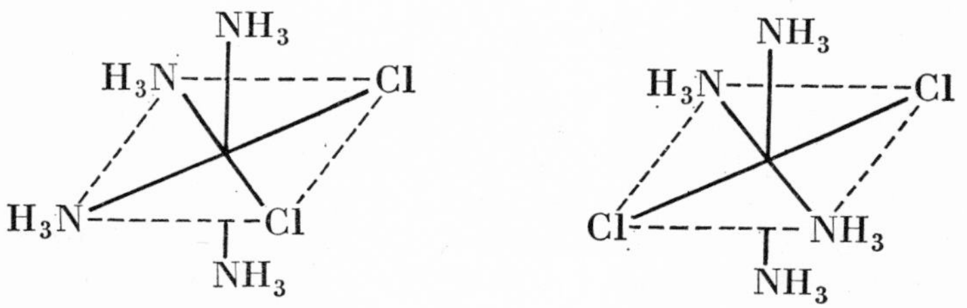

Cis (violet)   Trans (green)

FIGURE 2-1   Schematic representation of violet and green forms of [Co(NH₃)₄Cl₂]⁺ ion.

coordination theory that Werner proposed has not been discredited by time, but has served as a framework and a guide for all subsequent workers. His ideas have been extended; his observations have been explained or rationalized and have been shown to be compatible with modern theory. In this sense, Werner's contribution is a unique one. The fundamental pattern (or postulates) he proposed are as valid today as when they were presented over seventy years ago. This is true despite the tremendous advances in theory, despite the remarkable increase in the number of known coordination compounds, and despite the enormous volume of data concerning these compounds that has been accumulated.

* In this connection, it is interesting to note that Werner kept a sample of every compound prepared by himself or his students. These samples may be seen today at the University of Zurich.

There is an ironic aspect to Werner's contribution. Many persons gained the impression that he had answered all of the questions and that little remained to be done.[6] However, this impression has long since been overcome. We can read Werner's early papers and not disagree with any of his basic ideas. This unusual situation is a tribute to Werner, the man and the theory.

REFERENCES

1. O. Stallman, *J. Chem. Educ.*, **37**, 220 (1960).
2. J. C. Bailar, Jr., in "The Chemistry of the Coordination Compounds" (J. C. Bailar, Jr., ed.), Reinhold Publishing Corporation, New York, 1956, chap. 2.
3. W. Hückel, "Structural Chemistry of Inorganic Compounds," American Elsevier Publishing Company, New York, 1950, pp. 52–55, 85–89.
4. P. Pfeiffer, *J. Chem. Educ.*, **5**, 1090 (1928).
5. R. Wizinger-Aust, *Angew. Chem.*, **62**, 201 (1950).
6. R. S. Nyholm, *J. Chem. Educ.*, **34**, 166 (1957).

3 THE ARCHITECTURE OF COORDINATION COMPOUNDS

3-1 ISOMERISM: A BLUEPRINT FOR CHEMICAL ARCHITECTS

The years of understanding would logically follow the years of discovery. However, Werner's contribution, which made possible the years of understanding, was based upon his awareness of chemical structure or architecture. Thus it is worth while to examine the architecture of coordination compounds. A blueprint is an aid in appreciating the architecture of a building. Our blueprint for the appreciation of the architecture of coordination compounds is the study of isomerism.

During the infancy of chemical analysis, it was commonly believed that the properties of each substance depended upon its chemical composition. Thus, differences in the properties of two samples of the "same" substance were to be attributed to a difference in chemical composition. With the advent of highly accurate analyses, it became embarrassingly apparent that many compounds with the same chemical composition possessed different chemical and physical properties. Some differences can be attributed to polymorphism (different crystal forms), others to polymerism (relative number of atoms the same, absolute number different), but a large proportion of the cases are to be attributed to isomerism (Greek: "equal weight"), which is caused by differences in the arrangement of the constituent parts, i.e., atoms.

Initially, isomerism was thought to be an exclusive property of organic compounds (and many persons still think that it is), but the complexity of even simple coordination compounds is such as to give rise to a variety of arrangements and, thus, isomers.

The concept of isomerism is one that seems to trouble most persons, and yet it is a phenomenon that is very familiar. Compounds, like words, are made up of components (atoms vs. letters); just as a given set of letters can be arranged in several ways, the atoms of a compound are subject to a variety of arrangements.

An important class of isomerism, known as stereoisomerism, arises from differences in the spatial arrangement of donor atoms coordinated to a central metal atom or ion. One of the two categories of stereoisomerism is *geometrical isomerism*, which is due to differences in the geometrical arrangement of the atoms. A second category is that of *optical isomerism*, which has its analogy close at hand, namely, the fact that the left hand is the mirror image of the right one; both are identical, but they cannot be superimposed. Of course, the classic analogy of optical isomerism is to be found in "Through the Looking-Glass" in the rotund twins, Tweedledum and Tweedledee. Also, many a visitor to a housing subdivision has discovered to his embarrassment that modern houses are frequently mirror images of each other.

Just as many houses, though similar in construction, fail to fall into neat categories, so do many isomers fail to fit into either category of stereoisomerism. The other types of isomerism are important and interesting, but they have been investigated less thoroughly than stereoisomerism. For the sake of convenience, we shall consider the other types of isomerism first and then look at stereoisomerism in more detail.

3-2   STRUCTURAL ISOMERISM: A STUDY IN PERMUTATIONS AND COMBINATIONS

The thorough classification of structural isomerism that was published posthumously by Werner[1] in 1920 is still used to good advantage. A disadvantage of Werner's thoroughness is that the number of types is overwhelming at first encounter. The classification that we shall present is somewhat different, but reference will be made to Werner's system for those who wish to pursue the subject in more detail.

Most of the examples of structural isomerism are the result of permutation and combination of ligands and metal atoms. If spatial arrangements enter in, then, of course, there is an overlap with stereoisomerism. Structural isomerism arises because of different distributions of ligands within and outside the coordination sphere, because of different distributions of a set of ligands about two or more coordination centers, and because of ligand isomerism. All the isomers in each of the three types of structural isomerism differ in chemical and physical properties.

Coordination-sphere Isomerism

This isomerism occurs since coordinating solvent molecules (Werner's *solvate* isomerism) or ions (Werner's *ionization* isomerism) can be either inside or outside the coordination sphere. Although water is the most common coordinating solvent, others, such as amines and alcohols, are surely to be expected.

Coordination-sphere isomerism is exemplified by the three forms of $CrCl_3 \cdot 6H_2O$ which are assigned the formulas

$$[Cr(H_2O)_4Cl_2]Cl \cdot 2H_2O$$
$$[Cr(H_2O)_5Cl]Cl_2 \cdot H_2O$$
and $\qquad [Cr(H_2O)_6]Cl_3$

These isomers differ in their chemical and physical properties (the colors are respectively green, blue-green, and violet). The first and second isomers are obtained by warming a dilute hydrochloric acid solution of the third.

If an ion is the cause of coordination-sphere isomerism, the isomers have the same molecular weight but yield different ions in solution. A good example of this is the isomeric pair

$$[Co(NH_3)_5Br]SO_4 \quad \text{(dark violet)}$$

and

$$[Co(NH_3)_5SO_4]Br \quad \text{(red or red-violet)}$$

A solution of the dark violet salt does not yield a precipitate of silver bromide upon the addition of silver nitrate solution, but a precipitate of barium sulfate is formed when barium chloride is added; a solution of the red isomer behaves in the converse manner.

A slight permutation is involved in what Werner called *valence* isomerism. For example, the following pair

$$[(H_3N)_5Cr\overset{H}{\leftarrow}O—Cr(NH_3)_5]X_5$$

and

$$[(H_3N)_5Cr—O—Cr(NH_3)_5]X_4 \cdot HX$$

differ formally only in that H^+ is inside or outside the coordination sphere, but the two salts do have different properties.

Distribution Isomerism

A given set of ligands can be distributed between two or more coordination centers in a variety of ways. The isomers may have the same molecular weight (Werner's *coordination* isomerism) or different molecular weights (Werner's *polymerization* isomerism). Coordination centers, a minimum of two, are usually divided between a cation and an anion, but they may be present in a multinuclear complex (*coordination-position* isomerism). Distribution isomerism thus represents a "choosing-up" process.

For example, two different ligands A and B can be distributed between two metals M and M'. Two limiting isomers $[MA_6][M'B_6]$ and $[M'A_6][MB_6]$, as well as intermediate arrangements, $[MA_3B_3][M'A_3B_3]$, in addition to many others, could be expected. Examples of this are the two compounds having the formula $CoCr(NH_3)_6(CN)_6$. Both are yellow and only slightly soluble in water, but their method of preparation differs:

$$[Co(NH_3)_6]Cl_3 + K_3[Cr(CN)_6] \rightarrow 3KCl + \underline{[Co(NH_3)_6][Cr(CN)_6]}$$
$$[Cr(NH_3)_6]Cl_3 + K_3[Co(CN)_6] \rightarrow 3KCl + \underline{[Cr(NH_3)_6][Co(CN)_6]}$$

Distribution isomerism appears to be involved in the interesting behavior of $HgAg_2I_4$. At 45°C this compound is reversibly transformed from a red to a yellow form, apparently because of a thermally induced shift in the position of the ions and a change in coordination about the metal ions, as indicated by the equation

$$AgHg[AgI_4] \rightleftharpoons Ag_2[HgI_4]$$
$$\text{Red} \qquad \text{Yellow}$$

The structures of the two forms are presented elsewhere.[2]

The metal ions or coordination centers need not be different, as indicated by the isomers

$$[Cr(NH_3)_6][Cr(NCS)_6]$$

and

$$[Cr(NH_3)_4(NCS)_2][Cr(NH_3)_2(NCS)_4]$$

When several coordination centers are present, isomers having different molecular weights can result. Several examples are known, and one set of isomers is listed in Table 3-1. The number of isomers is greater than is indicated because stereoisomers can also be expected for some of the examples.

Table 3-1 **SOME EXAMPLES OF THE DISTRIBUTION**
ISOMERS OF $Cr_n(NH_3)_{3n}(NCS)_{3n}$

Formula	Relative mol wt n
$[Cr(NH_3)_3(NCS)_3]$	1
$[Cr(NH_3)_6][Cr(NCS)_6]$	2
$[Cr(NH_3)_4(NCS)_2][Cr(NH_3)_2(NCS)_4]$	2
$[Cr(NH_3)_5NCS][Cr(NH_3)_2(NCS)_4]_2$	3
$[Cr(NH_3)_6][Cr(NH_3)_2(NCS)_4]_3$	4
$[Cr(NH_3)_4(NCS)_2]_3[Cr(NCS)_6]$	4
$[Cr(NH_3)_5NCS]_3[Cr(NCS)_6]_2$	5

Finally, a special but interesting situation arises when the coordination centers are a part of a multinuclear complex, as indicated by the isomeric pair

$$\left[(H_3N)_4Co \begin{matrix} & NH_2 & \\ \diagup & & \diagdown \\ & & \\ \diagdown & & \diagup \\ & O-O & \end{matrix} Co(NH_3)_2Cl_2 \right]^{++}$$

and

$$\left[Cl(H_3N)_3Co \begin{matrix} & NH_2 & \\ \diagup & & \diagdown \\ & & \\ \diagdown & & \diagup \\ & O-O & \end{matrix} Co(NH_3)_3Cl \right]^{++}$$

Ligand Isomerism

Of the many types of ligand isomerism, the simplest, donor atom isomerism (Werner's *structural isomerism*), is due to the fact that a coordinating agent, though behaving as a unidentate ligand, may contain more than one potential donor atom. For example, the thiocyanate ion $: \ddot{N}—\ddot{C}—\ddot{S} :^{-}$ might coordinate through either sulfur or nitrogen. Though coordination through the nitrogen atom is generally observed and some examples of attachment through the sulfur atom are reported, in each case only one form has been characterized. Similarly, thiosulfate ion,

$$
\begin{array}{c}
:\ddot{S}: \\
:\ddot{O}:\ddot{S}:\ddot{O}: \\
:\ddot{O}:
\end{array}
$$

might coordinate through either the sulfur or oxygen atom, but only that through sulfur has been reported. Coordination through the carbon atom to a single metal atom is indicated in carbon monoxide and cyanide ion.

The only authentic examples of donor atom isomerism are due to isomerism of the NO_2^- ion, which could involve coordination through oxygen (nitrito, ONO^-) or through nitrogen (nitro, NO_2^- form). Two isomers were prepared by Jörgensen:

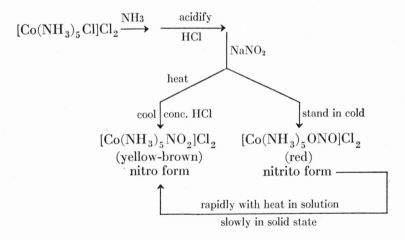

The structures were assigned on the basis of inference rather than evidence: The Co—N bond should be more stable; and compounds having six Co—N bonds have yellow-brown colors, but many having five Co—N bonds and one Co—O bond are red. In 1945, more sophisticated evidence (Debye-Scherrer x-ray patterns and ultraviolet absorption spectra) was presented that indicated that there was no isomerism, that only the nitro form existed, and that the red color was due to unreacted starting material. In 1956, still more sophisticated evidence (oxygen-tracer studies) was brought to bear on the problem, and this evidence supports the correctness of the original view.[3]

Ligand isomerism can arise because of *positional isomerism* within the ligand, e.g., the coordination compounds of 2-, 3-, or 4-methylpyridine:

Positional isomerism can also cause differences in the size of metal-chelate rings; an example is the metal chelates of 1,2- and 1,3-propanediamine:

The examples of isomerism noted in these sections serve to illustrate the complexities of the coordination compounds. The designation of the categories may seem to represent arbitrary distinctions, just like the designation of architectural styles according to location, but such categories serve to bring order out of the chaos caused by the myriad of compounds arising from the many possible combinations and permutations. However, many compounds fail to fit into the compartments of structural isomerism. The existence of two chemically different forms of $K_3Fe(CN)_6$ suggests that new types of isomerism may be involved. This may be true also of the red and green forms of $[Pt(NH_3)_4][PtCl_4]$.

There is room for expansion of the categories; there is need for the listing of new ones; and there are many isomers to be prepared or discovered.

3-3 STEREOISOMERISM: A STUDY OF ATOMS IN SPACE

Few chemists would deny that stereochemistry is one of the most interesting and exciting types of isomerism exhibited by coordination compounds. It is a vital and important type of isomerism because of its involvement in life processes. It is of historical interest because its existence was the keystone of Werner's coordination theory (Chap. 2).

As mentioned previously, stereoisomerism is of two types, geometrical and optical. Geometrical isomers differ in chemical and physical properties, but the properties of optical isomers (optical antipodes, enantiomers, mirror images) are nearly identical. Exceptions are the speed of reaction with other optical isomers and the direction of the rotation of the plane of plane-polarized light.

It might be well to see what we mean by the term "the plane of plane-polarized light." Ordinary light (Fig. 3-1) involves a wave motion with waves vibrating in plane A, in plane B, and in all the intermediate planes. Most of the planes of vibration are filtered out by certain substances such as tourmaline or Polaroid since they transmit only those waves of light which vibrate in the direction of their axes. If the beam of ordinary light is passed through a lens made of one of these substances (Fig. 3-1), the light which emerges is said to be *plane-polarized light.*

The effect of solutions of optical enantiomorphs on plane-polarized light may be studied with an instrument called a *polarimeter* (Fig. 3-2). A solution of a sample is placed in the sample tube, and the polarizer is rotated to the right or to the left until the maximum amount of light emerges. There are three possi-

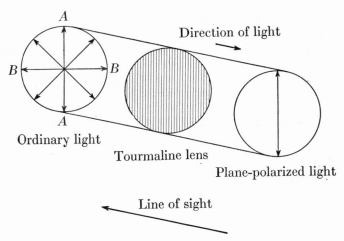

Direction of light

Ordinary light

Tourmaline lens

Plane-polarized light

Line of sight

FIGURE 3-1   Representation of the formation of plane-polarized light from ordinary light.

bilities: (1) rotation from the vertical is unnecessary—the sample is optically inactive;* (2) the lens is rotated to the right (i.e., the plane of plane-polarized light has been shifted to the right)—the sample is optically active (dextrorotatory or the *d* isomer); (3) the lens is turned to the left—the optically active sample is said

---

* This is not always true, because for some coordination compounds the degree and direction of rotation depends upon the wavelength of the light. Thus, a zero optical rotation at only one wavelength does not constitute proof of optical inactivity.

to be the *l* isomer (levorotatory). Under comparable conditions, the degree of rotation to the left by the *l* isomer of a given compound is exactly the same as that to the right by the *d* isomer.

Compounds that have the property of rotating the plane of plane-polarized light are said to be *asymmetric;* that is, they lack

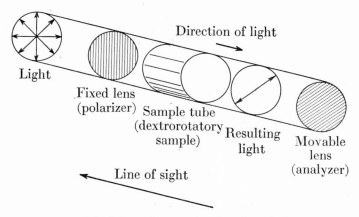

FIGURE 3-2   Schematic representation of a polarimeter.

symmetry. Another way of describing them is to say that their mirror images are nonsuperimposable. The elements of symmetry that make mirror images identical are a plane of symmetry, a center of symmetry, and an alternating axis of symmetry. If a compound possesses a plane of symmetry, the compound and its mirror image are identical (Fig. 3-3). The same statement is true for the other two elements of symmetry, but since they arise less frequently, they will not be discussed here.

With this background, we can consider stereoisomerism most conveniently by following the approach used elsewhere[1,4] and examining some of the possibilities for each important coordination number.

$cis\text{-}[\mathrm{Ma_4b_2}]$ $trans\text{-}[\mathrm{M(AA)_2b_2}]$

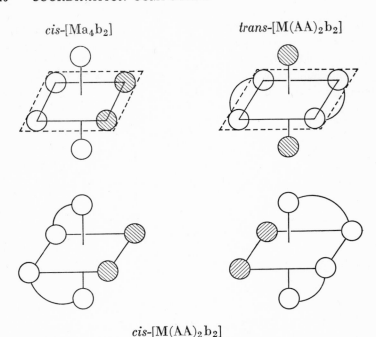

$cis\text{-}[\mathrm{M(AA)_2\,b_2}]$

FIGURE 3-3   Plane of symmetry in $cis\text{-}[\mathrm{Ma_4b_2}]$ and $trans\text{-}[\mathrm{M(AA)_2b_2}]$ (mirror image is superimposable) and lack of plane of symmetry in $cis\text{-}[\mathrm{M(AA)_2b_2}]$ (mirror image is not superimposable).

Coordination Number 2

The two bonds of the central atom can be directed collinearly or angularly. In either case, only one form is possible, as will be seen from the hypothetical examples:

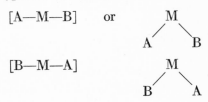

In each case, simple rotation of the lower form yields the top one.

Coordination Number 3

Two geometrical arrangements, planar and nonplanar (trigonal pyramidal), are possible for this uncommon coordination number, but stereoisomers have not been found. Geometrical

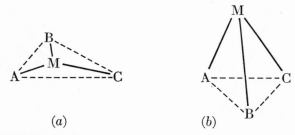

(a)   *(b)*

FIGURE 3-4   Some geometrical arrangements for coordination number three. (a) Unsymmetrical plane; (b) trigonal pyramid.

isomerism would be possible for an unsymmetrical trigonal plane, and optical isomerism would be predicted for compounds of the type [Mabc] having a trigonal pyramidal arrangement (Fig. 3-4).

Coordination Number 4

The four bonds of the central metal ion can lie in a plane or be directed tetrahedrally. In either case, certain compounds including those of the type [Ma$_4$] or [Mb$_4$], [Ma$_3$b] or [Mab$_3$], [M(AA)b$_2$], [M(AA)$_2$] [a and b are different unidentate groups; AA are bidentate groups or chelates (Table 1-1)] are each found in only one form. There are no stereoisomers because every possible arrangement is equivalent.

For compounds of the type [Ma$_2$b$_2$] no isomerism is noted for the tetrahedral case. For example, note that the two three-dimensional representations (Fig. 3-5) are "mirror images" and are identical and superimposable. If the five atoms of $[Ma_2b_2]$ lie in

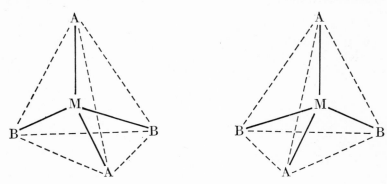

FIGURE 3-5 Tetrahedral arrangements of $[Ma_2b_2]$.

a plane, then two geometrical isomers (*cis*, adjacent; *trans*, opposite) are expected, as will be seen from the formulas:

The situation is somewhat more complicated for compounds of the type $[Mabcd]$. If a tetrahedral arrangement of bonds exists, two optical antipodes are predicted:

For a planar arrangement, three geometrical isomers are to be expected. These are indicated by the formulations and are distinguished by listing the arrangement of one atom in relation to each of the other three (Fig. 3-6).

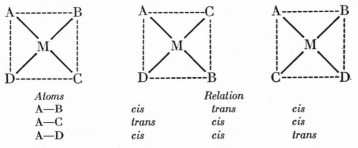

Atoms		Relation	
A—B	*cis*	*trans*	*cis*
A—C	*trans*	*cis*	*cis*
A—D	*cis*	*cis*	*trans*

FIGURE 3-6   Isomeric forms of [Mabcd], planar configuration.

Three such isomers have been obtained for the compound $[Pt(NH_3)(H_2NOH)(C_6H_5N)NO_2]NO_2$, and this fact has been used as experimental evidence that the arrangement of bonds (configuration) about the platinum(II) ion is planar.

The proof of configuration by the isomer-number method (comparison of number and type of isomers predicted with those found) has its pitfalls, the most obvious being the need for skilled synthetic chemists. Two such chemists, Mills and Quibell,[5] used another very ingenious approach, which involved preparing iso-butylenediamine*meso*-stilbenediamine-platinum(II) cation as follows:

$$\begin{array}{c} H_2C-NH_2 \\ | \\ (CH_3)_2C-NH_2 \end{array} + K_2PtCl_4 \rightarrow \begin{array}{c} H_2C-NH_2 \\ | \qquad\quad \diagdown \\ \qquad\qquad PtCl_2 \\ | \qquad\quad \diagup \\ (CH_3)_2C-NH_2 \end{array}$$

$\downarrow$ *meso*-stilbenediamine

$$\left[\begin{array}{cc} H_2C-NH_2 & H_2NCHC_6H_5 \\ | \quad\diagdown\;\diagup & | \\ & Pt \\ | \quad\diagup\;\diagdown & | \\ (CH_3)_2C-NH_2 & H_2NCHC_6H_5 \end{array} \right]^{++}$$

The planar configuration would lack a plane of symmetry, and optical isomers would be expected. If the platinum(II) ion has a tetrahedral arrangement of bonds, the entire molecule would have a plane of symmetry since the plane of symmetry of the diphenyl ring coincides with the plane of the dimethyl ring (Fig. 3-7).

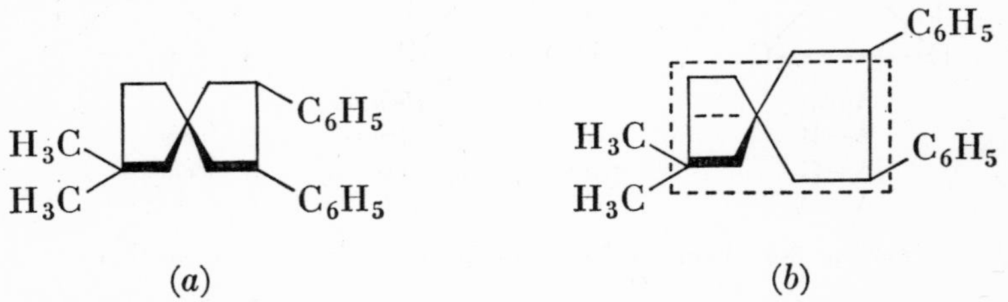

(a)   (b)

FIGURE 3-7   Possible configurations of the compound [M(AA)(BC)]. (a) Planar, no plane of symmetry; (b) tetrahedral, plane of symmetry.

Although the obtaining of optical antipodes was regarded as the proof of the planar arrangement, it is only fair to point out, as Mills and others have done, that this experiment really shows that the tetrahedral arrangement is definitely excluded. The chemical evidence per se does not eliminate the pyramidal arrangement.

Coordination Number 5

Until recently, there were very few authentic examples of coordination compounds which exhibited the coordination number of 5. There are now a number of examples of such compounds, but no cases of stereoisomerism have been established, although these would be expected. Some of the possible geometrical forms are shown in Fig. 3-8.

Coordination Number 6

Compounds with elements exhibiting a coordination number of 6 have been widely studied, and the knowledge of stereoisomerism is probably the greatest for this coordination number. With a few exceptions, there is no physical or chemical evidence for an arrangement other than octahedral.

It is interesting to look at the chemical evidence because it is

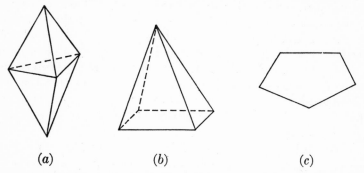

(a) (b) (c)

FIGURE 3-8 Possible geometrical forms for a coordination number of five. (a) Trigonal bipyramid; (b) tetragonal pyramid; (c) pentagonal plane.

based upon the isomer-number method. The three plausible ways of arranging six coordinating groups about a central metal atom are indicated in Fig. 3-9. In each of these arrangements all positions are equivalent.

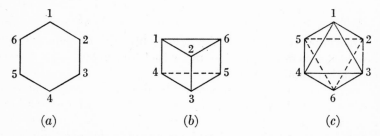

(a) (b) (c)

FIGURE 3-9 Possible geometrical forms for coordination number six. (a) Hexagonal plane; (b) trigonal prism; (c) octahedron.

Let us consider the isomers expected for each form for the compounds of the following types:

[Ma$_6$], [Ma$_5$b], [Mab$_5$].   Only one form is predicted, regardless of the arrangement.

[Ma$_2$b$_4$].   For a planar or trigonal prism arrangement, three geometrical isomers (due to "a" groups being at points 1 and 2, or at 1 and 3, or at 1 and 4), are expected, but the octahedral arrangement would lead to two isomers: *cis* ("a" atoms at adjacent vertices: 1 and 2 or 2 and 3, etc.) and *trans* ("a" atoms at opposite vertices: 1 and 6 or 2 and 4, etc.). Since two and only two isomers have ever been isolated, it is tempting to conclude that the octahedral arrangement is the correct one. Of course, it can be argued that this is negative evidence (perhaps chemists just haven't been able to isolate that third isomer).

[Ma$_3$b$_3$].   Compounds of this type are not of much help because, again, three isomers are predicted for the hexagonal plane and trigonal prism forms. Two isomers ("face": "a" atoms at positions 1,2,3; and "edge": "a" atoms at positions 1,3,6) are predicted for the octahedral arrangement, and, again, only two forms have been isolated.

[M(AA)$_3$].   Assuming that bidentate groups, AA, can only occupy adjacent or *cis* positions, then one form is expected for a planar arrangement, two geometrical isomers are predicted for the trigonal prism arrangement, and a pair of optical isomers is to be expected if the geometry is octahedral. The separation of a number of compounds of the [M(AA)$_3$] type into optical enantiomorphs provided conclusive proof of the octahedral arrangement for coordination number 6.

Werner was able to separate (or resolve) the enantiomers of *cis*-[Co(H$_2$NCH$_2$CH$_2$NH$_2$)$_2$(NH$_3$)Cl]$^{++}$. This ought to have been convincing proof of the correctness of his prediction of optical isomerism among six-coordinate compounds. However, his critics argued that the optical activity was due to the presence of carbon atoms. We now recognize that this was a ridiculous argument, but at that time carbon compounds were strongly associated with the concept of optical activity. With characteristic ingenuity, Werner prepared and resolved the multinuclear complex ion[6]

$$\left[Co \left(\begin{array}{c} H \\ O \\ \diagdown \\ O \\ H \end{array} Co(NH_3)_4 \right)_3 \right]^{6+}$$

which is devoid of carbon atoms, and this silenced his critics.

Much of the stereochemistry of coordination number 6 is beyond the scope of this treatment. It is worth mention that many of the stereoisomeric possibilities have not been realized because of experimental and synthetic inadequacies. The magnitude of the problem becomes staggering, particularly when we consider that for a compound of the type [Mabcdef] 15 pairs of enantiomorphs can be expected, but we can become encouraged by the fact that at least five of the isomers expected for

$$[Pt(py)(NH_3)(NO_2)IClBr]$$

have been prepared.[7]

Coordination Numbers Greater Than Six

The occurrence and geometry of compounds involving higher coordination numbers (seven, eight, and nine) have been described elsewhere.[8,9] The likely geometrical arrangements and the possible isomers for these coordination numbers have been considered in detail by other authors.[10]

3-4 STEREOCHEMISTRY, FUNCTION AND DESIGN

One of the trends in modern architecture is the emphasis on function and design. The same trend is to be observed in the architecture of coordination compounds. Stereoisomerism is of interest because of its function in biochemistry, in synthesis, and in theoretical studies. Knowledge of the role of stereoisomerism in these fields enables chemists to design ligands and coordination compounds to perform desired functions.

Biochemical Implications

Biochemistry, the study of the chemistry of living organisms, is an area in which stereochemistry is of great importance. For example, the proteins of the human body are formed entirely from L-amino* acids, $RCH(NH_2)COOH$. Just why the D isomers are excluded has yet to be answered, but coordination compounds might be involved (page 55).

The importance of stereochemistry is also indicated by an observation of Dwyer and coworkers.[11] The compound

$$[Ru(o\text{-phen})_3](ClO_4)_2†$$

causes death when introduced into mice by peritoneal injection, but the toxic dose of the *d* isomer is about one-half that of the *l* isomer. Despite this, when the *l* isomer is added to the *d* form, the time of death is delayed slightly. These results are clearly due to the complex ion, and not to free Ru^{++}, because the complex ion is not decomposed by strong acid or by strong base. Further examples of the role of metal ions and coordination compounds in biochemistry can be found elsewhere.[12]

---

* The letters *d*- and *l*- refer to the direction of rotation, whereas the letters D- and L- refer to the configuration of the isomer.

† $[Ru(o\text{-phen})_3](ClO_4)_2 = \left[\begin{array}{c} \end{array} Ru \right] (ClO_4)_2 .$

Application to Synthesis

The stereochemical effects in biochemistry may be due to the presence of optically active ligands in coordination compounds. A study of these compounds has been made by Bailar and his co-workers,[13] and two examples of their work will indicate the applications to synthesis and biochemistry.

The first example is that of an asymmetric synthesis (Fig. 3-10), i.e., a process which produces an optically active compound

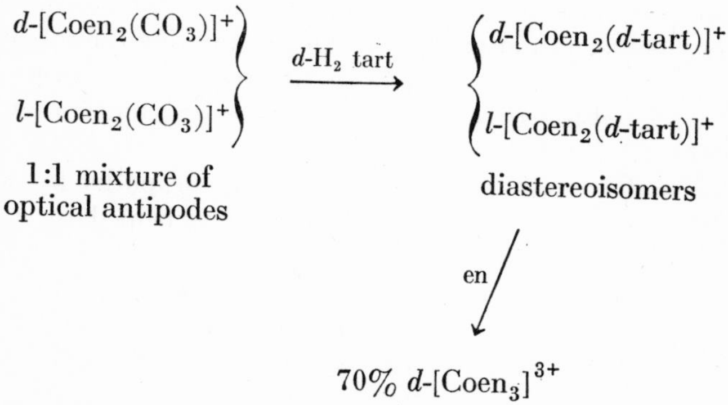

$$
\left. \begin{array}{l} d\text{-}[Coen_2(CO_3)]^+ \\[1em] l\text{-}[Coen_2(CO_3)]^+ \end{array} \right\} \xrightarrow{d\text{-}H_2 \text{ tart}} \left\{ \begin{array}{l} d\text{-}[Coen_2(d\text{-tart})]^+ \\[1em] l\text{-}[Coen_2(d\text{-tart})]^+ \end{array} \right.
$$

1:1 mixture of
optical antipodes

diastereoisomers

en $\Big/$

$$70\% \ d\text{-}[Coen_3]^{3+}$$

FIGURE 3-10   An example of an asymmetric synthesis. en = $H_2NCH_2CH_2NH_2$; H_2tart = $HOOCCH(OH)CH(OH)COOH$; pn = $H_2NCH_2CH(CH_3)NH_2$.

by means of an optically active reagent. The reaction of d-tartaric acid with cis-$[Coen_2CO_3]^+$ results in a pair of diastereoisomers, which do not differ greatly in solubility. However, separation is effected by treatment with ethylenediamine and the yield of d-$[Coen_3]^{3+}$ is about 70 per cent of that expected.

This interesting result suggested the separation of dl mixtures of optically active acids (tartaric, lactic, and others). Indeed, it was found that d-$[Co(l\text{-}pn)_2CO_3]^+$ reacts preferentially with the dextro antipode in a 1:1 dl mixture of the organic acid. In this instance, the coordination compound behaves in a manner that is analogous with that of some enzymes. Both the coordination compound and the enzyme may react preferentially with one optical antipode and thus separate the *dl* mixture. They differ in that the enzyme destroys one optical antipode, whereas the coordination compound preserves and removes the antipode.

Theoretical Studies

Coordination compounds are frequently used as "models" to test theories. For example, the means by which electrons are exchanged in oxidation-reduction reactions has been the subject of much discussion. An interesting means of studying the rate of exchange between osmium(II) and osmium(III) is based on the fact that it is related to the rate of loss of optical activity of a mixture of d-$[Os(dipy)_3]^{++}$ and l-$[Os(dipy)_3]^{3+}$.[14]

Our understanding of the mechanisms or paths by which reactions of coordination compounds occur is helped by stereochemistry. It serves as a bridge between what we observe (macrochemical observation) and what the molecules must be doing (microchemical inference). For example, the loss of optical activity with time can be correlated with the rate of reaction (cf. page 86):

$$l\text{-}[Coen_2Cl_2]^+ + X^- \rightarrow dl\text{-}[Coen_2ClX]^+ + Cl^-$$

Finally, stereochemistry is of historical significance not only because its very existence was a major factor in the acceptance of Werner's coordination theory, but because it helped to bring about what might be called the age of understanding.

Architecture is an ever-changing field, and we can but guess at the direction it will take in the future. A similar statement can be made about the architecture of coordination compounds, except that we can make a more intelligent guess. The stereochemistry of higher coordination numbers will be commonplace. The function and design aspects of stereochemistry will receive great emphasis. The use of stereochemistry in synthesis will become better understood, with consequent enlightenment regarding its biochemical implications.

REFERENCES

1. T. Moeller, "Inorganic Chemistry," John Wiley & Sons, Inc., New York, 1952, pp. 247-252.
2. G. L. Clark, "Applied X-Rays," 4th ed., McGraw-Hill Book Company, Inc., New York, 1955, p. 516.
3. R. K. Murmann and H. Taube, *J. Am. Chem. Soc.*, **78**, 4886 (1956).
4. W. C. Fernelius, in "Chemical Architecture" (R. E. Burk and O. Grummitt, eds.), Interscience Publishers, Inc., New York, 1948, pp. 53-100.
5. W. H. Mills and T. H. H. Quibell, *J. Chem. Soc.*, **1935**, 839.
6. A. Werner, *Ber.*, **47**, 3087 (1914).
7. L. N. Essen et al., *C.A.*, **51**, 12732 (1957); **55**, 2194, 21955, 24353 (1961).
8. T. D. O'Brien, in "The Chemistry of the Coordination Compounds" (J. C. Bailar, Jr., ed.), Reinhold Publishing Corporation, New York, 1956, pp. 392-397.
9. R. J. Gillespie, in "Advances in the Chemistry of the Coordination Compounds" (S. Kirschner, ed.), The Macmillan Company, New York, 1961, pp. 34-49.
10. L. E. Marchi, W. C. Fernelius, and J. P. McReynolds, *J. Am. Chem. Soc.*, **65**, 329 (1943).
11. F. P. Dwyer et al., *Nature*, **170**, 190 (1952).
12. N. J. Seven, ed., "Metal-binding in Medicine," J. B. Lippincott Company, Philadelphia, 1960.
13. J. C. Bailar, Jr., *Record Chem. Progr. (Kresge-Hooker Sci. Lib.)*, **10**, 17 (1949).
14. F. P. Dwyer and E. C. Gyarfas, *Nature*, **166**, 481 (1950).

4 THE YEARS OF UNDERSTANDING

It might seem artificial to make a distinction between the years of discovery and the years of understanding because we are still involved in both periods. Actually, the differentiation is real and valid because the years of understanding form a separate and distinct period. As we have noted, Werner's discovery and contribution were so enormous and so overwhelming that many scientists were left with the false impression that nothing more remained to be discovered. This was the common pattern, though, to be sure, there were oases of active and fertile investigations.

In a general way, the years of understanding can be divided into three periods in which the means of understanding were based on chemical methods, on physical methods, and on theoretical approaches. The change in approach from chemical to theoretical represents an increased sophistication which has been possible because of increased understanding. The increased degree of sophistication has been accompanied by a tremendous increase in the cost of research. It is well to remember that Werner and his coworkers were able to conduct their research using test tubes, beakers, and the simplest kind of physical chemical equipment. It is worth noting that the same thing can still be done.

We shall review the years of understanding by considering the three periods or approaches.

4-1 CHEMICAL METHODS

Much of Werner's initial work at Zurich was done in the old laboratories which were popularly and descriptively known as "the catacombs." Four chemical methods were used by Werner and his students: identification of ions, the *cis* placement-replacement principle, the isomer-number method, and *trans* elimination.

Identification of Ions

This method has been mentioned in previous chapters (pages 6 and 38). While simple and perhaps obvious, it does provide much useful information. The fact that the combination $Na_3Fe(CN)_6$ does not show the usual tests for cyanide ions would indicate that all are bound to the ferric ion; sodium ion, but not ferric ion, responds to the usual tests. As noted earlier (page 27) the formulas for the cobalt(III) chloride–ammonia combinations (Table 2-1) are derived on the basis of the gram moles of silver chloride readily precipitated. Further examples are mentioned in Chap. 3 (pages 38 ff.).

The *Cis* Placement-Replacement Principle

The structure of *cis* and *trans* isomers can be deduced by means of *cis* placement-replacement principles. First of all, the placement of a bidentate ligand must be *cis;* i.e., the donor atoms must be in adjacent positions. *Trans* spanning (Fig. 4-1) usually is not possible* because of the short distance between the two donor atoms. The *cis* placement-replacement principle can be simply stated: "A *cis* isomer will result if a bidentate ligand is

---

* *Trans* spanning is theoretically possible *if* the separation of the two donor atoms is sufficiently great. There are claims that *trans* spanning has occurred, but the structures proposed are speculative.

replaced by two unidentate ligands, assuming that no rearrangement occurs."

The *cis* placement-replacement principle was used by Werner and his students on many occasions. As an example, the violet

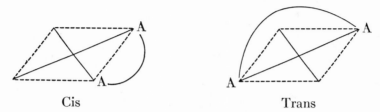

Cis   Trans

FIGURE 4-1 Examples of spanning by a bidentate ligand.

form of $[Co(NH_3)_4Cl_2]^+$ (page 33) was shown to be the *cis* isomer because it was prepared by treating $[Co(NH_3)_4CO_3]^+$ with HCl in alcohol.

The assumption that no rearrangement occurs in *cis* replacement often has not been justified. For example, if

$$[Coen(NH_3)_2CO_3]^+$$

is treated with alcoholic hydrogen chloride, two chloride ions enter in adjacent positions, whereas treatment with dilute hydrochloric acid results in the *trans* dichloro compound (Fig. 4-2). Thus while the *cis* placement-replacement principle is useful, it has limitations.

Isomer-number Methods

This method consists in comparing the number and kind (nonstereoisomeric, geometric, optical) of isomers found with those expected for various possible arrangements. Several examples of the use of this method have been given in Chap. 3.

The obvious disadvantage of the method is the need for luck or experimental excellence on the part of the chemist in order to find all the isomers. Another disadvantage is encountered with optical isomers; the need to remove the resolving agent* has caused difficulties in the past. Platinum(II) ion, generally agreed to have

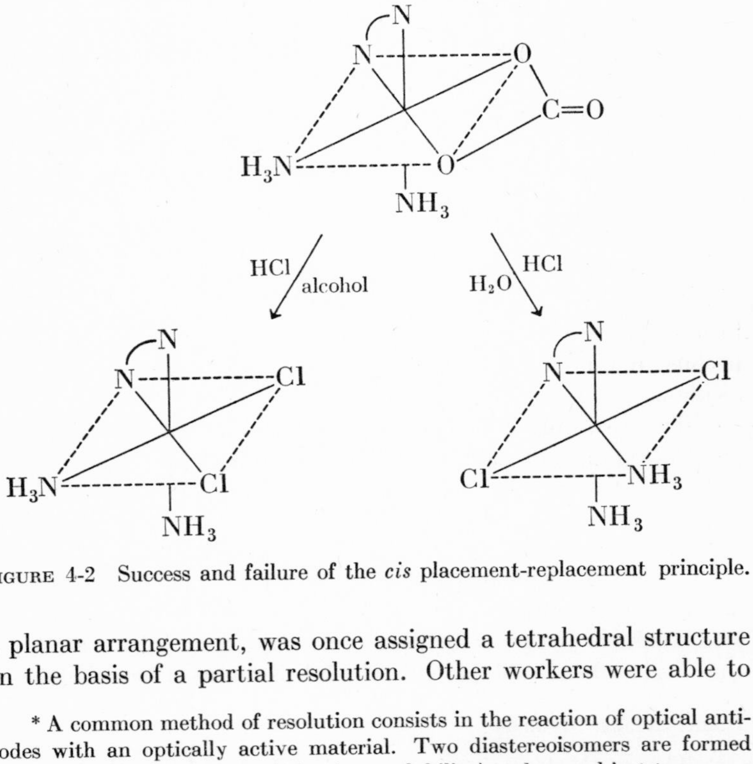

FIGURE 4-2   Success and failure of the *cis* placement-replacement principle.

a planar arrangement, was once assigned a tetrahedral structure on the basis of a partial resolution. Other workers were able to

* A common method of resolution consists in the reaction of optical antipodes with an optically active material. Two diastereoisomers are formed which differ in physical properties (e.g., solubility) and are subject to separation. The resolving agent is removed from each of the separated diastereoisomers, and the resolved optical antipodes are obtained. For organic compounds, the resolving agent is an optically active acid or base. For coordination entities an optically active ion of opposite charge is used. Obviously, for neutral coordination compounds, other methods such as preferential adsorption on an optically active solid must be used.

demonstrate that the optical activity was not due to a tetrahedral structure but only to an impurity.

Trans Elimination

This concept has been applied with great success to square planar complexes, especially those of platinum(II). It is found that ligands differ in their influence on groups in the *trans* position. This influence involves either the weakening of the metal-ligand bond directly opposite or a directing of the entry of a group into the *trans* position.

The *trans* effect or elimination was suggested by Werner to rationalize the reactions of two forms of $Pt(NH_3)_2Cl_2$.* The existence of two isomeric forms caused Werner to suggest the square planar structure (isomer-number basis, page 49) and that the isomers were the *cis* and *trans* forms. Werner did not seem to recognize the generality of *trans* elimination, though it has been extensively used in recent years.

In addition to its use in distinguishing between *cis* and *trans* isomers, *trans* elimination is used as a guide to the synthesis of square planar compounds. For example, the *trans*-directing ability of nitrite ion exceeds that of chloride ion and treatment of

$$PtCl_3NO_2{}^{2-}$$

with ammonia results in *trans-*, not *cis-*,

$$PtCl_2(NO_2)NH_3{}^-$$

---

* The reactions described by Jörgensen and the explanation given by Werner are clearly presented by other authors.[1]

4-2 PHYSICAL METHODS

Paralleling the advance of chemistry as measured by the development of schools of chemistry there is an advance in the use of physical methods. These are methods that depend upon properties which are apparent to the senses. They range from the simple and obvious, such as color, to the sophisticated, such as paramagnetic relaxation phenomena.

Preliminary Identification

All the compounds were characterized by their colors and named according to these colors (page 16), which was logical in view of the highly colored nature of most coordination compounds. Also, molecular-weight data were commonly determined and still are.

Conductivity

The formulas for many coordination compounds suggested that they should be electrolytes. Conductivity studies were used to show that the expected number of ions were present. These studies brought out the manner in which the charge on the coordination sphere depends on the number of coordinated anions. The relationship is effectively demonstrated in Fig. 4-3, which shows the variation of molar conductivity (related to the number of ions present) as a function of the number of chloride ions coordinated to platinum(II). In general, conductivity studies were and are of great help in understanding the structure of coordination compounds (for example, see page 27). At times, the method seemed to fail because more ions were formed than expected. For example, the dark green salt, $[Co(NH_3)_4Br_2]Br$, dissolved to give a dark green solution the conductivity of which rapidly increased. At the same time the color of the solution changed, finally becoming red, the color expected for $[Co(NH_3)_4(H_2O)_2]Br_3$. Werner and Miolati[2] suggested that these changes were due to *aquation*, the displacement of the bromide ion from the coordination sphere by water:

$$[Co(NH_3)_4Br_2]Br + 2H_2O \rightarrow [Co(NH_3)_4(H_2O)_2]Br_3$$

Though care is needed in applying the conductivity method to study of coordination compounds, useful results have been obtained. The results obtained by Werner and Miolati were invaluable in supporting Werner's coordination theory.

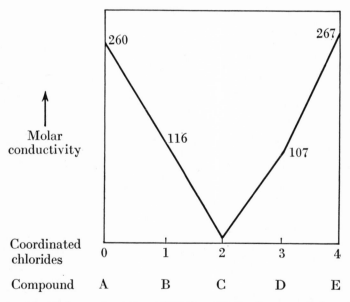

FIGURE 4-3 Molar conductivity at 1000 liters dilution for some platinum(II) compounds. A, $[Pt(NH_3)_4]Cl_2$; B, $[PtCl(NH_3)_3]Cl$; C, $[PtCl_2(NH_3)_2]$; D, $K[PtCl_3(NH_3)]$; E, $K_2[PtCl_4]$.

X-ray Studies

Valuable information regarding the distribution and direction of bonds around a coordinated metal ion can be obtained from the use of x-rays. These studies are very useful since they yield data concerning the sizes of the ions or molecules in a crystal, as well as the distances and angles between them. However, the existence of an ion in the solid state does not necessarily imply its existence in solution. Thus x-ray studies may reveal the existence of coordination compounds that do not exist in solution because of instability.

An important limitation of the x-ray method is that its value is dependent upon the completeness of the study. The work is both slow and tedious, and short cuts have led to serious errors. X-ray studies are best limited to single crystals since complicated crystals often do not yield complete data. Generally, complicated structures have not been determined. Complete structures are not realizable for compounds containing hydrogen because the hydrogen atom is too small for detection by x-rays. The presence of a heavy metal as a central atom can be an advantage,* since it is readily detected by x-rays and thus establishes a point of reference. However, the presence of very heavy metal atoms may also tend to obscure the position of light atoms.

Occasionally, it may not be possible to prepare single crystals, and it is necessary to use crystalline powders. Although the patterns obtained are often not as sharp, this method is simple and convenient. Studies of powders may be used in the identification of unknown substances by comparison of the x-ray pattern obtained with patterns of known substances.

Magnetochemistry

Magnetic behavior is caused by the motion of electrons about the nucleus and is similar to the flow of current in a loop of wire

---

* The determination of structures of the divalent metal-phthalocyanine compounds is a good example of this.[3]

which also results in a magnetic effect. There are three sorts of magnetic behavior noted for chemical substances, depending upon what happens when the substance is placed in a magnetic field: (1) the attraction will be tremendous (*ferromagnetism*) if the substance has a lattice of particles with electrons having parallel spins, as with iron; (2) mild repulsion will occur (*diamagnetism*) if there are no unpaired electrons; or (3) mild attraction will be noted (*paramagnetism*) if unpaired electrons are present. Paramagnetism increases with increasing number of unpaired electrons.

Thus, studies of magnetic behavior can indicate the number of unpaired electrons. A further value of magnetic studies or magnetochemistry is the possibility of being able to infer the valence of the metal ion, the bond type, and the geometry of the coordination compounds. For example, if a tetracoordinate nickel(II) compound is diamagnetic, it is reasonable to conclude that the four bonds are square planar. If the same compound is paramagnetic (two unpaired electrons), a tetrahedral arrangement is indicated, but not conclusively so.

Dipole Moment

A molecule which is nonsymmetrical is said to be a dipole and to possess a permanent electric moment, or dipole moment. As applied to coordination compounds, dipole-moment measurements can be of value in distinguishing between isomers of a compound, particularly between *cis* and *trans* isomers. Obviously, a *trans* isomer is more symmetrical than a *cis* isomer, and its dipole moment, if any, is lower. Unfortunately, dipole-moment measurements must be made in a nonpolar solvent; this requirement eliminates salts and limits study to the relatively few soluble, neutral complexes. For example, *trans*-$[PtCl_2(AsR_3)_2]$ (where R = C_2H_5-) has a dipole moment of about zero, whereas the value for the *cis* isomer is about eleven debye units.[6]

Other Methods

These include studies of color and absorption spectra (absorption of light as a function of wavelength), the use of isotopes and exchange reactions, and the use of such recent tools as nuclear magnetic and electron spin resonance. Examples and discussion of these and other physical methods have been presented by other authors.[4-6]

4-3 THEORETICAL APPROACHES

The contributions made by various theories[7] constitute a very important aspect of the years of understanding. Each contribution is part of a cycle: A theory is advanced in an attempt to rationalize the known facts and to predict future trends. There follows a period of very active and inspired research which is designed to prove or to disprove the current theory. In either case, progress results and with it the increased understanding that shows the flaws, the shortcomings, of the theory. At this point a new theory is developed and a new cycle begins.

It seems to us that three periods of theoretical development can be distinguished: the Werner-Lewis-Sidgwick period, the years in which the Pauling theory has held sway, and the era of ligand field theory. Concurrent with the periods of theoretical development, there were studies of solution behavior of coordination compounds that resulted in the accumulation of important data. All periods and theories have in common certain desires and goals. The hallmarks of a successful theory would include its ability to rationalize the stability of a coordination compound, predict its geometry, and predict or rationalize many of its chemical and physical properties (particularly the color). It should do all these things in a quantitative manner. Let us look at the three periods and see how nearly the above goals were attained.

The Werner-Lewis-Sidgwick Period

The first theoretical approach was the Werner coordination theory. This was probably not a theory in the modern sense of the word, because modern theory is concerned with problems of a degree of subtlety and sophistication far beyond Werner's dreams. Though Werner's theory was accepted in nearly every particular, to Werner's dying day there was great dissatisfaction with certain aspects. Much of the disagreement centered about the concept of two valences. In short, there was a need for the development of a theory of bonding in coordination compounds.

A major contribution was made in 1916 by G. N. Lewis, who suggested that the covalent bond consisted of a pair of electrons shared by two atoms. Each atom might contribute one electron to the pair or one atom might contribute both. The latter corresponds to Werner's secondary valences, and the suggestions of Lewis did much to clarify Werner's[7] concept of two valences.

Beginning in 1923 further contributions were made by N. V. Sidgwick, who suggested the term coordinate, or dative, bond for a linkage that was formed when a donor atom supplied an electron pair to be shared with a metal atom or ion. The coordinate covalent bond was represented by an arrow pointing from the donor atom. The covalent character of the bond was presumed to be the cause of the stability and definite geometry of the compound. Using this theory, Sidgwick was able to rationalize many of Werner's observations.

An obvious flaw of the theory is that metals characteristically lose electrons, and accepting a share of many electron pairs would cause the metal ion to have a formal negative charge. This paradox was considered by Linus Pauling, who is given credit for suggesting a solution.

Pauling's Contributions[8,9]

Pauling has made many contributions to modern theory, three of which are pertinent to our discussion.

1. He suggested that the formal negative charge on the metal could be relieved by double bonding (or π bonding) between the metal ion and certain ligands, e.g., CN^-, CO, NCS^- (Fig. 4-4).

$$A: \longrightarrow M \qquad\qquad A: \longrightarrow M$$

$$:N\equiv C: \overline{Fe} \qquad\qquad :\overline{\underset{..}{N}}=C=Fe$$

$$(a) \qquad\qquad\qquad (b)$$

FIGURE 4-4   Representation of (*a*) Sidgwick coordinate bond and (*b*) Pauling double bond.

Electrons are donated by the ligand, and the ligand accepts a share of the electrons of the metal. In this way, the formal negative charge is spread over many atoms instead of being concentrated.

2. The geometry expected for different coordination numbers was explained by a concept termed *orbital* hybridization.* Apparently, one *s* orbital and three *p* orbitals of an atom combine to form four sp^3 hybrid bonds that are stronger than if these orbitals were used alone. These four equivalent bonds, characteristic of carbon, are directed toward the corners of a regular tetrahedron. Similarly, a square planar arrangement would involve dsp^2 hybridization; an octahedral one, d^2sp^3 hybridization.

3. Pauling demonstrated the applicability of magnetochemistry to the inference of bond type and geometry of coordination compounds. A few examples should illustrate the method (Table 4-1).

There appeared to be two types of iron(III) compounds: (1) $[FeF_6]^{3-}$, which was decomposed into F^- and Fe^{3+} in water and

---

* We can regard the electron as being a charged particle in motion about a positively charged nucleus. The motion results in electron density patterns or *orbitals* which have characteristic shapes (Fig. 4-5).

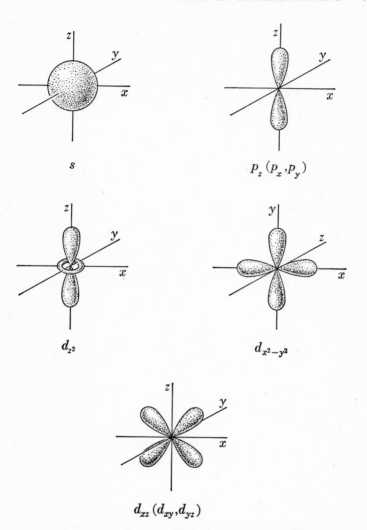

FIGURE 4-5 Atomic orbitals (not drawn to scale).

which had five unpaired electrons in the $3d$ level of iron, and (2) $[Fe(CN)_6]^{3-}$, which was inert in water and which had only one unpaired electron (based on magnetic behavior). The electron distributions, then, would be 1*a* and 1*b*, respectively, for $[FeF_6]^{3-}$ and $[Fe(CN)_6]^{3-}$, and it was suggested that the first compound involved ionic bonding and was an "ionic" complex whereas the second was "covalent."

The greater stability of cobalt(III) complexes over those of cobalt(II) was explained by noting that the latter would have one electron in the $5s$ orbital where it could be readily removed to form a cobalt(III) derivative.

Pauling predicted,[10] on the basis of theoretical arguments, that the coordination compounds of divalent nickel that had been observed to be diamagnetic (example 3*b*, Table 4-1) would have a square planar arrangement. This arrangement was later observed for many diamagnetic nickel(II) compounds.

Copper(II) complexes were found to have one unpaired electron, but the magnetic criterion is not applicable to these compounds. If arrangement 4*a* (Table 4-1) were involved, a tetrahedral geometry would be expected, but since the geometry is planar, electron distribution 4*b* is written. Unfortunately, such a distribution should suggest that one electron could be removed to form a copper(III) compound, and this is not observed. Arrangement 4*c* was suggested for certain copper(II) compounds, and this overcomes some of the difficulties.

The main advantages of the Pauling theory are its simplicity and its ability to provide reasonable, qualitative explanations. In many ways, it has rendered valuable service to the understanding of coordination compounds. With the greater insight permitted by the theory, it was realized that the theory could not interpret the colors of coordination compounds, and some other flaws became apparent. One unsatisfactory result was the misleading assignment, based on magnetic studies, into "covalent" and

Table 4-1 ELECTRON DISTRIBUTION AND MAGNETOCHEMISTRY OF SOME TRANSITION–METAL IONS

Ion	Electron distribution					Comment based on magnetochemistry
	3d	4s	4p	4d	5s	
1a Fe(III)	↑ ↑ ↑ ↑ ↑	□	□ □ □	□ □ □ □		"Ionic," "outer-orbital," "high-spin"
1b Fe(III)	↑↓ ↑↓ ↑ ↑ ↑	□	□ □ □	*		"Covalent," "inner-orbital," "low-spin"
2a Co(II)	↑↓ ↑↓ ↑↓ ↑ ↑	□	□ □ □			
2b Co(III)	↑↓ ↑↓ ↑↓ ↑ ↑	□	□ □ □			
3a Ni(II)	↑↓ ↑↓ ↑↓ ↑ ↑	□	□ □ □		↑	Tetrahedral (?)
3b Ni(II)	↑↓ ↑↓ ↑↓ ↑ ↑	□	□ □ □		□	Square planar
4a Cu(II)	↑↓ ↑↓ ↑↓ ↑↓ ↑	□	□ □ □			
4b Cu(II)	↑↓ ↑↓ ↑↓ ↑↓ ↑	□	□ □ ↑			
4c Cu(II)	↑↓ ↑↓ ↑↓ ↑↓ ↑	□	□ □ □	□ □ □ □		

*The brackets enclose the orbitals that are presumably involved in bonding.

"ionic" compounds. Also, the theory failed to predict the geometry of certain four-coordinate compounds.

Ligand Field Theory

Some of these problems that the Pauling theory was not designed to cover were overcome by adoption of *ligand field theory*. Although a modification of this theory was used to good advantage by physicists in the 1930s, its usefulness escaped most chemists until about 1951.

The theory pictures a coordination compound in simplest terms as a metal ion surrounded by charged or partially charged ligands (electric dipoles). The ligands provide an electric environment (or field) for the metal ion, and the environment affects certain electrons (specifically, those present in the partially filled *d* orbitals). In the absence of the electric environment all the electrons are equal (same energy level); within the environment some electrons are "more equal than others," that is, two different energy levels result, one higher, one lower than the original. The number of electrons in each level, and the difference between the two levels depends upon the nature of the environment. This in turn depends upon the arrangement of the ligands about the metal ion and the tendency of the ligands to donate their electron pairs.* This is represented in Fig. 4-6.

Ligand field theory offers several advantages. It is basically simple and permits a quantitative approach to coordination chemistry. The theory does not require a connection between magnetic properties and structure, but it does permit a meaningful connection to be made between the color of a complex and its structure.

---

* A ligand (e.g., CN^-) having a strong tendency to donate its electron pair results in a "strong field," a greater difference between the two levels, and a pairing of the electrons of the metal ion (a "low-spin" or "inner-orbital" compound results). The other extreme is represented by fluoride ion which has a low tendency to donate an electron pair. (A weak field and a "high-spin" or "outer-orbital" compound results.)

This, then, is a review of the years of understanding which have been made possible by the application of all three approaches. The years of understanding are yet with us and make possible a

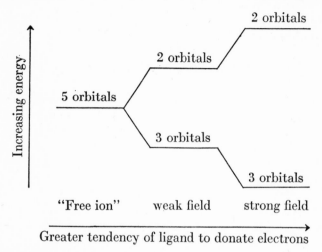

FIGURE 4-6   Representation of variation of d-orbital energy levels with electric environment in an octahedral complex. Each orbital can accept two electrons. The "two orbitals" are the d_{z^2} and the $d_{x^2-y^2}$; the "three orbitals" are the d_{xy}, d_{xz}, d_{yz} orbitals.

new age of discovery. A historian of the future will no doubt regard the present years as very exciting ones and record that they were years of great change, perhaps even years of transition. Assuming this to be so, it might be well to take stock of past trends and possibly suggest future ones; this we shall do in the next chapter.

REFERENCES

1. F. Basolo and R. G. Pearson, "Mechanisms of Inorganic Reactions," John Wiley & Sons, New York, 1958, chap. 4.
2. A. Werner and A. Miolati, Z. physik Chem., **12**, 33 (1893).

3. J. M. Robertson, *J. Chem. Soc.*, **1935**, 615.
4. R. C. Brasted and W. E. Cooley, in "The Chemistry of the Coordination Compounds" (J. C. Bailar, Jr., ed.), Reinhold Publishing Corporation, New York, 1956, pp. 563–624.
5. L. E. Orgel, "Introduction to Transition Metal Chemistry," Methuen & Co., Ltd., London, 1960.
6. A. E. Martell and M. Calvin, "Chemistry of the Metal Chelate Compounds," Prentice-Hall, Inc., Englewood Cliffs, N.J., 1952, chap. 7.
7. L. E. Sutton, *J. Chem. Educ.*, **37**, 198 (1960).
8. L. Pauling, "The Nature of the Chemical Bond," 3d ed., Cornell University Press, Ithaca, N.Y., 1960.
9. L. Pauling, *J. Chem. Educ.*, **39**, 461 (1962).
10. L. Pauling, *J. Am. Chem. Soc.*, **53**, 1367 (1931).

5

COORDINATION COMPOUNDS IN SOLUTION

5-1 INTRODUCTION

A very important aspect of the world of coordination compounds is the behavior of these substances in solution, their formation and reactions. The importance of solution chemistry is apparent when we consider that it embraces much of the known coordination chemistry. Historically, past workers have been concerned first with equilibria and later with the mechanisms of inorganic reactions. For the sake of convenience, we shall consider these two areas separately and discuss the generalizations or trends that have been discerned. Since this is a final chapter, it seems appropriate to suggest areas that will probably receive attention in the future.

5-2 COORDINATION COMPOUND EQUILIBRIA

Quantitative information is obtained by determining the *stability* or *formation constants*. The term *stability* refers to the amount of association that occurs in solution between two species in a state of equilibrium. Qualitatively, the greater the association, the greater the stability of the compound that results. Quantitatively, the magnitude of the equilibrium (stability, or formation) constant for the association expresses the stability. This constant is expressed in powers of 10, usually a positive number, and thus is the inverse of the so-called instability constant frequently encountered in qualitative analysis. If the species are a metal ion M and a ligand A (omitting charges for the sake of convenience) the coordination compound MA_n might be expected to form in solution. The compound MA_n is not formed exclusively; rather, the compound is formed in a stepwise manner through a series of equilibria. These stepwise equilibria were first shown in 1941 by Bjerrum and Leden, working independently. This advance revived the study of formation constants of metal complexes, which had been carried on intermittently since 1902.

The equilibria involved represent the displacement by the ligand of solvent molecules from the coordination sphere of the metal ion. We can represent the equilibria involved and the formation constants associated with each as follows:

1. $M + A \rightleftharpoons MA \qquad K_1 = \dfrac{(MA)^*}{(M)(A)}$

2. $MA + A \rightleftharpoons MA_2 \qquad K_2 = \dfrac{(MA_2)}{(MA)(A)}$

$n.$ $MA_{n-1} + A \rightleftharpoons MA_n \qquad K_n = \dfrac{(MA_n)}{(MA_{n-1})(A)}$

When M is a nickel(II) ion and A is ammonia, the complex ion $[Ni(NH_3)_6]^{++}$ can form, six stepwise equilibria can be detected, and six constants can be measured.

A common method for measuring formation constants is a potentiometric titration of a solution of a ligand (such as a β-diketone or an amine present as a perchlorate salt) and a metal ion by a standard solution of base. From measuring the concen-

* ( ) indicates the concentration of the species expressed in gram moles per liter.

tration of ligand, metal ion, and titrant and the pH of the solution, and knowing the basicity (measured similarly, in the absence of metal ions) of the ligand, the constant for each step can be calculated. A potentiometric titration experiment which illustrates the determination of formation constants is described by Goldberg.[1]

Once the constants have been determined, what do they mean? The magnitude of an individual constant indicates the stability of the species, its tendency to form, and the comparison of the various constants that have been determined permits quantitative statements concerning trends and generalities.

A number of trends have been noted,[2] and the following are typical.

Each succeeding ligand is accommodated less readily than the previous one. This is true for most metal ions and most ligands and is exemplified by the copper compounds listed in Table 5-1.* It has a statistical and a charge-attraction basis. If there are N places for a ligand, it is a more favorable situation than if there are $N - 1$ or $N - 5$ places. Also, with the placement of successive ligands the charge decreases or is spread over a larger volume and offers less attraction to electron donors. There are exceptions to the generalization, e.g., silver ion–amine complexes (Table 5-1).

Table 5-1   **FORMATION CONSTANTS, LOG K_n, FOR METAL ION–AMINE COMPLEXES**

n	Cu^{++}		Ag$^+$	
	NH$_3$	H$_2$NCH$_2$CH$_2$NH$_2$	NH$_3$	H$_2$NCH$_2$CH$_2$NH$_2$
1	4.0	10.7	3.19	4.7
2	3.2	9.3	3.83	
3	2.7			
4	2.0			

* A summary of formation constant data has been compiled by Bjerrum, Schwarzenbach, and Sillén.[3]

The Chelate Effect

Ethylenediamine complexes are relatively more stable than ammonia complexes, and in general, a chelate compound is more stable than one involving unidentate ligands. For copper we can compare the constants involved in placing two nitrogen donors about the copper ion:

$$
\begin{array}{ccc}
\mathrm{H_3N}\diagdown & & \mathrm{H_2C}{\overset{\overset{\displaystyle \mathrm{H_2}}{N}}{\diagdown}} \\
\searrow\mathrm{Cu^{++}} & \text{or} & |\mathrm{Cu^{++}} \\
\mathrm{H_3N}\diagup & & \mathrm{H_2C}\underset{\underset{\displaystyle \mathrm{H_2}}{N}}{\diagup}
\end{array}
$$

i.e., we should compare $\log K_1 + \log K_2$ for ammonia (7.2) with $\log K_1$ for ethylenediamine (10.7). If this is done, the ethylenediamine compound is clearly more stable. The ethylenediamine derivative of silver is less stable than that of the ammine (4.7 vs. 6.96). This is probably due to the strain of the chelate ring (cf. page 3).

The Number of Points of Attachment

Related to the chelate effect is the fact that the stability of a metal-chelate compound increases with the number of points of attachment, though the stability per donor atom may remain constant (Table 5-2). The lessened stability of $(\mathrm{H_2NCH_2CH_2})_3\mathrm{N}$ complexes is probably due to the conflict between a metal such as copper(II) ion, which usually exhibits a planar configuration, and a ligand that requires a distorted tetrahedral arrangement of bonds. On the other hand, zinc(II) ion, which frequently exhibits a tetrahedral configuration, forms a more stable complex with

$$(\mathrm{H_2NCH_2CH_2})_3\mathrm{N}$$

than with

$$\mathrm{H_2NCH_2CH_2NHCH_2CH_2NHCH_2CH_2NH_2}$$

Table 5-2 EFFECT OF THE NUMBER OF POINTS OF
ATTACHMENT ON THE STABILITY OF
SOME COPPER(II) POLYAMINE
COMPOUNDS

Amine	$\log K$	$(\log K)/N$†
$H_2N\ NH_2$*	10.7	5.35
$H_2N\ NH\ NH_2$	16.0	5.33
$H_2N\ NH\ NH\ NH_2$	20.4	5.1
$(H_2N)_3N$	18.8	4.7

*⌒ = —CH_2CH_2—.
† N represents the number of nitrogen atoms in the amine.

($\log K$ values are 14.6 and 11.8). This appears to be an example
of a "lock-and-key" arrangement which leads to stability.

Basicity of the Ligand

The coordinating tendency of a ligand is frequently a direct
function of the basicity of the ligand. This is not very surprising
because the attraction for a positive metal ion should parallel the
attraction for a hydrogen ion. This presumes that size or electronic
factors are not involved; they often are.

The Metal Ion

Most of the attention has centered on ligand properties and
not on those of the metal ion. For a wide variety of ligands and a
series of divalent metal ions, there is a relatively invariant order
of stability: Mn < Fe < Co < Ni < Cu > Zn. This is the Irving-
Williams order, so named for the English chemists who have called
attention to it.[4] An extended series of relative stabilities includes
both nontransition and transition divalent metal ions: Pd > Hg >
UO_2 > Be > Cu > Ni > Co > Pb > Zn > Cd > Fe > Mn >

Mg > Ca > Sr > Ba. This is an order of stabilities that is subject to variation with the ligand.

An awareness of these and other trends permits workers to select the proper ligand or coordination compound for a given function or to design better ligands. In addition, formation constants are frequently of value in understanding coordination processes. A good example of this is the study of 1-nitroso-2-naphthol:

$$O{=}N:$$

This is an effective precipitating agent for cobalt(II) ion, and it is used by chemists to separate cobalt from nickel, though these ions have similar chemical properties.

Obviously, there must be some marked difference in the behavior in solution of the two coordination compounds. The equilibria involved were studied using dioxane-water* as a solvent. The data obtained for the cobalt(II) and nickel(II) titrations are

Table 5-3   FORMATION CONSTANTS, LOG K_n, FOR
1-NITROSO-2-NAPHTHOL IN 75 VOL.
PERCENT DIOXANE-WATER
AT 30°C

	Cobalt(II)	Nickel(II)
log K_1	10.67	10.75
log K_2	12.14	10.54
log K_3		6.80

* The metal chelates are insoluble in water but soluble in dioxane. Since equilibria cannot be studied in pure dioxane, a compromise is adopted, and 75 volume percent dioxane–25 volume percent water is used.

listed in Table 5-3. A number of interesting points emerge from this[5] and other studies.

1. Previous workers concluded that 3.25, not just three or two, molecules of 1-nitroso-2-naphthol were used in coordination with each cobalt(II) ion.

2. Only two formation constants are observed for the cobalt(II) compounds, and log K_2 is greater than log K_1, which is anomalous.

3. In the cobalt(II) determination, not all the ligands could be accounted for; 1.25 were "missing." Five molecules of ligand had been added for every cobalt(II) ion to insure equilibrium conditions. Of the five, two were involved in coordination (as indicated by the release of two protons) in an acidic region, and in a basic region, 1.75 molecules of noncoordinated ligand were neutralized. Thus, of five molecules, 3.75 were accounted for, 1.25 were missing.

A reasonable explanation of the results has been suggested.[5] First, reaction of cobalt(II) ion with two molecules of ligand represented as

$$Np \overset{\displaystyle NO}{\underset{\displaystyle OH}{<}}$$

liberates two hydrogen ions.

$$Co^{++} + 2Np\overset{\displaystyle NO}{\underset{\displaystyle OH}{<}} \rightarrow [Co(Np\overset{\displaystyle NO}{\underset{\displaystyle O}{<}})_2] + 2H^+ \quad (1)$$

Second, in the alkaline solution but not in acid, the cobalt in the coordination compound is oxidized by some of the excess ligand:

$$1[\mathrm{Co(Np} \overset{\diagup \mathrm{NO}}{\underset{\diagdown \mathrm{O}}{}})_2] + 1.25\mathrm{Np} \overset{\diagup \mathrm{NO}}{\underset{\diagdown \mathrm{OH}}{}} \rightarrow$$

$$1[\mathrm{Co(Np} \overset{\diagup \mathrm{NO}}{\underset{\diagdown \mathrm{O}}{}})_2]^+ + 0.25\mathrm{Np} \overset{\diagup \mathrm{NH_2}}{\underset{\diagdown \mathrm{OH}}{}} + 0.25\mathrm{H_2O} + 1\mathrm{Np} \overset{\diagup \mathrm{NO}}{\underset{\diagdown \mathrm{O^-}}{}} \qquad (2)$$

Finally, another coordination reaction occurs:

$$[\mathrm{Co(Np} \overset{\diagup \mathrm{NO}}{\underset{\diagdown \mathrm{O}}{}})_2]^+ + \mathrm{Np} \overset{\diagup \mathrm{NO}}{\underset{\diagdown \mathrm{O^-}}{}} \rightarrow [\mathrm{Co(Np} \overset{\diagup \mathrm{NO}}{\underset{\diagdown \mathrm{O}}{}})_3] \qquad (3)$$

Thus, the missing 1.25 ligands are really present. However, the hydrogen ions associated with these ligands are consumed in the reduction process [Eq. (2)] and are not available for titration. For this reason it is not possible to determine log K_3. The "odd" requirement of *3.25* ligands per cobalt ion is now reasonable: 0.25 molecule of ligand is involved in the oxidation of each cobalt [Eq. (2)] and three molecules are required to form

$$\mathrm{Co(Np} \overset{\diagup \mathrm{NO}}{\underset{\diagdown \mathrm{O}}{}})_3$$

[Eqs. (1) and (3)].

Separation of nickel(II) ion is possible because nickel forms a soluble anion,

$$[Ni(Np \overset{NO}{\underset{O}{\diagup}})_3]^-$$

whereas the cobalt compound,

$$[Co(Np \overset{NO}{\underset{O}{\diagup}})_3]$$

is neutral and is insoluble in water.

5-3 MECHANISMS OF REACTIONS IN SOLUTION

A mechanism is a theory, a model, that is proposed to explain how a reaction occurs. As such, the model cannot be proved; it can be shown to be reasonable, moderately or exceptionally so. When given the choice of several models, the "best" one is taken to be the one that is the simplest which is capable of explaining all or most of the known facts. A model becomes outmoded when more facts are presented that cannot be accommodated.

Reaction mechanisms have a theoretical interest, but they are of great practical importance because they represent an attempt to change synthetic chemistry from an art to a science. Too often the procedure used to prepare a coordination compound is exactly the same as that described by Jörgensen or Werner more than sixty years ago. Frequently these methods are recipes rather than procedures. A knowledge of reaction mechanisms permits a logical, often successful, approach to the synthesis of a desired compound.

One important series of reactions, called substitution reactions (nucleophilic), involves the replacement of one ligand by another. Other types of reactions include electron transfer or oxidation-reduction, electrophilic substitution (in which a metal ion attacks a coordinated ligand), and isomerization reactions (which are often nucleophilic substitution reactions). In nucleophilic substitution, the attacking species, a ligand, is electron-rich, and is called a *nucleophile* (or nucleophilic reagent) because it seeks, as it were, a positively charged species. Thus, nucleophilic substitution, abbreviated S_N, may be represented as

$$Y: + MR_nX \rightarrow MR_nY + X:$$

where $Y:$ is a nucleophilic reagent.

In simplest terms, nucleophilic substitution could occur in two ways: by a dissociation or by an association mechanism. The dissociation mechanism involves a slow step, one which determines the rate of the reaction, in which a ligand is lost. This is followed by a very rapid combination of the nucleophilic reagent and the dissociated coordination entity, $MR_n{}^+$:

$$MR_nX \longrightarrow MR_n{}^+ + X{:}^- \qquad \text{(slow)}$$
$$MR_n{}^+ + Y{:}^- \rightarrow MR_nY \qquad \text{(fast)}$$

Since the rate of the reaction depends only upon the concentration of MR_nX, the mechanism is called unimolecular and is abbreviated S_N1 (substitution nucleophilic unimolecular). The association mechanism differs in that the intermediate coordination species has a higher coordination number:

$$MR_nX + Y: \xrightarrow{\text{slow}} Y \cdots MR_n \cdots X \xrightarrow{\text{fast}} MR_nY + X:$$

Since the slow, or rate-determining, step is proportional to the concentration of two species, the mechanism is abbreviated S_N2 (substitution nucleophilic bimolecular).

This terminology was originally devised in connection with organic reaction mechanisms and was later applied to the reactions of coordination compounds. The similarity of terminology has been unfortunate to the extent that it has suggested analogous behavior where none exists. A good example of this is the distinction that has been made between *cis-trans* and *d-l* conversions in both organic and inorganic chemistry. In organic chemistry, a *cis-trans* change

Trans   Cis

is a fundamentally different process from a *d-l* change:

$$d\text{-}\ R'\!-\!\overset{\displaystyle R}{\underset{\displaystyle R''}{\overset{|}{\underset{|}{C}}}}\!-\!Br + OH^- \quad \rightarrow \quad l\text{-}\ HO\!-\!\overset{\displaystyle R}{\underset{\displaystyle R''}{\overset{|}{\underset{|}{C}}}}\!-\!R' + Br^-$$

By contrast, in coordination chemistry, *cis-trans* and *d-l* conversions can be described by the same model, i.e., edge-displacement,[6] and thus need not be fundamentally different. This model involves considering a substitution reaction of a compound [Coen$_2$AX] by a nucleophile, Y:. X is a ligand that is being replaced and A is a reference group which serves to define the position of X (*cis, trans, d* or *l*). The substitution process is represented by the equation (omitting the positions of the ethylenediamine groups for clarity):

The position of the reference determines the identity of the complex. For example, if A is in position 1, the starting compound is a *cis* isomer, the product a *trans* compound. If A is at position 2, the change is a *trans-cis* one. If the reference group is at position 3 or 4, the process is a *d*-to-*l* or *l*-to-*d* conversion. The important point to note is that for all cases the process of substitution is the same.

It is quite beyond the scope of this volume to review the developments in the study of the reactions of coordination compounds in solutions, but this has been done elsewhere.[7]

5-4 A FUTURE WORLD OF COORDINATION COMPOUNDS

Having considered the many facets of coordination compounds from earliest times to the present, we might well inquire as to what we can expect of the future.

First of all, the present uses of ligands or coordination compounds will be more intensive and more extensive. One use, that of ion control, has become an important consideration in industrial processes because metal ions often have detrimental effects, such as the formation of insoluble materials or the catalysis of undesired reactions.

Ethylenediaminetetraacetic acid (EDTA) and the sodium salt are widely used as sequestering agents. About ten million pounds of EDTA and Na$_4$EDTA were produced in 1958; in 1935, the production was nil. Typically, EDTA is, or can be, added to liquid soap (haze prevention), to hydrogen peroxide (prevention of catalytic decomposition), to boiler feed waters (water softening, removal of calcium ion), and to wines (for turbidity prevention). Ferric EDTA is added to iron-deficient soils to overcome chlorosis in citrus trees; ordinary iron compounds form insoluble materials in these soils. A calcium EDTA complex has been successfully used in the treatment of lead poisoning. Developments such as these will undoubtedly continue.

We can expect to see new and extended generalizations presented. These will probably emerge from explorations of design and functions of ligands. Little is known of the solution behavior of ligands containing arsenic or phosphorus donor atoms, for example, yet it is known that ligands having such donor atoms do form stable and interesting coordination compounds. New generalizations and new ligands will undoubtedly lead to new uses of these compounds.

The subject of solution behavior suggests the importance of a knowledge of the mechanisms of the reactions of coordination compounds. Much has been accomplished in this field;[7] the keen interest in it suggests a future of significant contributions. An obvious contribution is that the synthesis of many coordination compounds will become a science, whereas it is now an art. As our knowledge of reaction mechanisms increases, there must be corresponding advances in theoretical aspects, and our present views will be reexamined in the light of new information.

With the increased understanding of solution behavior will come a greater insight into the role of coordination compounds in asymmetric syntheses, enzymatic reactions, and biochemical processes in general. Perhaps the results in this area will have the most significance; certainly they will be of great interest because of their implications for the individual person. There is interest in the role of coordination entities in the origin of life. Currently, there is the problem of storing oxygen for use by astronauts, a problem that must be solved before any protracted journey into space can be undertaken. One solution is to use, or copy from, green plants, which utilize chlorophyll and sunlight to convert carbon dioxide (which we exhale) and water to starch with the liberation of oxygen. Unless someone finds a coordination compound to fill the role of chlorophyll, the first space ship will either contain tanks of oxygen or resemble a greenhouse.

With the insight which the preceding advances should permit, there will be parallel technological advances. These will give man more effective control over his environment and better understanding of his world, which is in reality a world of coordination compounds.

REFERENCES

1. D. E. Goldberg, *J. Chem. Educ.*, **39**, 328 (1962); **40**, 341 (1963).
2. Cf. A. E. Martell and M. Calvin, "Chemistry of the Metal-Chelate Compounds," Prentice-Hall, Inc., Englewood Cliffs, N.J., 1952, chaps. 4 and 5.
3. J. Bjerrum, G. Schwarzenbach, and L. G. Sillén, "Stability Constants," pts. I and II, *Chem. Soc.* (*London*) *Spec. Publ.* **6, 7** (1957–1958).
4. H. Irving and R. J. P. Williams, *J. Chem. Soc.*, **1953**, 3192.
5. C. M. Callahan, W. C. Fernelius, and B. P. Block, *Anal. Chem. Acta*, **16**, 101 (1957).
6. D. D. Brown, C. K. Ingold, and R. S. Nyholm, *J. Chem. Soc.*, **1953**, 2674.
7. F. Basolo and R. G. Pearson, "Mechanisms of Inorganic Reactions," John Wiley & Sons, Inc., New York, 1958.

APPENDIX   Preparation of Tetrahedral

and Octahedral Models

The principles of isomerism discussed in Chaps. 2 and 3 are more easily understood when three-dimensional models are available. An octahedron and a tetrahedron can be prepared by copying the patterns shown in Fig. A-1 and Fig. A-2 and assembling according to the following directions.

DIRECTIONS:

Copy the patterns, using stiff paper. Fold down on all lines and join edge 1 to edge 1, edge 2 to edge 2, etc. Fasten edges with glue or transparent tape.

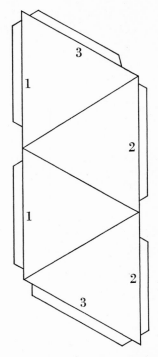

FIGURE A-1   Pattern for a tetrahedron.

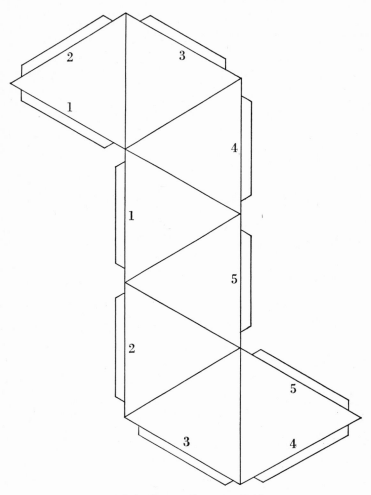

FIGURE A-2 Pattern for an octahedron.

INDEX

DATE DUE

	JUL 2 3 2009		